# Dictionary of Human Resource Management

# Dictionary of Human Resource Management

Gurpreet Randhawa

ATLANTIC
PUBLISHERS & DISTRIBUTORS (P) LTD

Published by

**ATLANTIC**

**PUBLISHERS & DISTRIBUTORS (P) LTD**

7/22, Ansari Road, Darya Ganj,
New Delhi-110002
Phones : +91-11-40775252, 23273880, 23275880, 23280451
Fax : +91-11-23285873
Web : www.atlanticbooks.com
E-mail : info@atlanticbooks.com

Branch Office
5, Nallathambi Street, Wallajah Road,
Chennai-600002
Phones : +91-44-64611085, 32413319
E-mail : chennai@atlanticbooks.com



Printed in India at Nice Printing Press, A-33/3A, Site-IV, Industrial Area, Sahibabad, Ghaziabad, U.P.

# Preface

The *Dictionary of Human Resource Management* is a comprehensive and useful dictionary which provides up-to-date information on the various aspects of human resource management (HRM). The department of HRM in an organisation provides significant support and advise to line managers. The attraction, preservation and development of high calibre personnel are a source of competitive advantage for the business. State-of-the-art management tools with cutting edge innovations are increasingly being adopted in the context of the vast materials and measures that are arrayed within the horizons of human endeavour.

The *Dictionary of Human Resource Management* encompasses various concepts, terms, applications, innovations and ideas that together constitute human resource management functions in an organisation. It has been prepared keeping in mind the requirements of management students of both undergraduate and postgraduate levels along with researchers and teachers in the field of Master of Business Administration (MBA). Special care has been taken to present the various terms of HRM in a simple language and lucid manner for an easy understanding by the readers. This dictionary also includes the important US acts and terms relating to HRM. Wherever necessary, the abbreviations are also given after the headword. An asterisk (*) placed at the end of a term indicates that it can be looked up for further details or explanation in the dictionary.

Surely, it will prove to be a useful, comprehensive, practical and intelligent companion to the students, researchers and teachers of HRM. It will also be beneficial to all those who are working in an organisation, particularly those responsible for the management of human resources.

I am thankful to Dr. K.R. Gupta, Hon. Advisor, Atlantic Publishers & Distributors (P) Ltd. for seeing this book through to press.

**Gurpreet Randhawa**

# A

**AAP.** Abbreviation for Affirmative Action Plan.*

**Ability.** An employee's competence in performing a job.

**Ability to pay.** A concept of wage payment which considers that wage level must be based on an organisation's ability to pay.

**Absenteeism.** The unauthorized absence from work. The failure of an employee to come to work when he is scheduled to work. It has become a major problem in most of the organisations. As a remedial measure, organisations are introducing attractive incentive schemes, flexible working hours and increased annual leaves.

**Absolute judgment.** A performance appraisal format in which the supervisor is asked to make judgments about an employee's performance based solely/only on performance standards. Under this format, no comparisons to the performance of coworkers are made.

**Abusive dismissal.** A dismissal in which a worker is dismissed in a legally and technically correct way, however in doing so the management has abused its powers.

**Accelerating vocational training.** A training program which intends to provide help to employees so that they acquire skills, which were traditionally acquired by apprenticeship training, in a much shorter period than taken by apprenticeship program. Usually, these kind of training programs are sponsored by government.

**Acceptance authority theory.** A theory which states that formal authority has no significance until and unless it is accepted by the subordinates. Authority of a superior is meaningless unless it is accepted by his subordinates.

**Accident.** An unexpected or chance event, usually which causes damage.

**Accident book.** A book maintained by almost every employer in an organisation in order to keep a record of any personal injury suffered by the employees due to an accident at workplace.

**Accident frequency rate.** Usually calculated as the number of lost time accidents per 100,000 man-hours worked.

**Accident insurance.** An insurance policy in which the policyholder would get a particular amount of money in case of his accident. And in case of the death of the policyholder in an accident, then his dependants would be paid.

**Accident prevention.** A program followed in the organisations in order to prevent or at least reduce the occurrence of accidents at the workplace. Includes steps like effective supervision, proper training and proper maintenance of machinery, etc.

**Accident proneness.** The tendency of a person to cause more number of accidents than an average.

**Accountability.** The obligation of a person in carrying out his responsibility and exercise authority according to standards established by the supervisor or superior. It is a person's liability for proper discharge of his duties.

**Accrued benefits.** The benefits due under a pension scheme.

**Achievement motivation theory.** A theory of needs, developed by David McClelland and his associates, that focuses on three basic motivation needs: achievement, power and affiliation. **Need for achievement** refers to individual's drive to excel and strive to succeed. **Need for power** is concerned with exercising influence and control. **Need for affiliation** refers to the desire for friendly and close interpersonal relationships.

**Achievement tests.** Tests which are designed to measure the level of knowledge, skills and abilities already achieved by the candidates. For example, knowledge of English, etc.

**Action learning program.** It is a on-the-job training method. In this, the management trainees are allowed to work full-time on the projects, analyzing and solving problems in other departments.

**Action plan.** A written document which consists of steps that the manager and the trainee will take in order to ensure that the training transfers to the job. In detail, an action plan includes particular dates and timings when the trainee and manager agree to meet for discussing the progress being made in utilizing the learned capabilities and skills on the job.

**Action skill.** Ability to carry out skillfully the desired behaviour in a particular situation. For example, in a T-group training. *See T-group training*.

**Action steps.** A written affirmative plan to be developed by an employer to show their plans to reduce the underutilization of the protected groups. In U.S., the employers with federal contracts must develop a complete list of action steps. For example, a firm can inform job openings for minority groups and females by publishing its affirmative plan.

**Active crops of executives.** An organisation of executives who are still working. Also, they voluntarily offered their expertise in various operational aspects of the business.

**Active practice.** The actual or real performance of job-related duties and tasks by the trainees during their training period.

**Activity.** A term used to describe the work required to complete a particular event or a task.

**Actuary.** An individual who is expert/trained in calculating rates of insurance.

**Acuity.** A person's ability to discriminate fine detail in using one of the senses. For example, in hearing, vision, etc.

**ADA.** Abbreviation for Americans with Disabilities Act.*

**Added hours.** When the workers work overtime then the amount paid to them is calculated by adding hours to the normal working week for which a worker is paid.

**Additional voluntary contribution (AVC).** An additional amount paid by an employee (in excess of the amount desired under the contract of employment) into an approved occupation pension scheme. The aim of the employee is to raise the amount of pension payable.

**Adhoc.** For a specific or particular situation. For a limited period. For example, an organisation hire adhoc employees for six months or one year period.

**Adhoc committee.** A committee formed for a specific purpose and may be dismissed after the completion of a particular task.

**Adhoc mail survey.** A type of mail survey in which the questionnaire is sent to persons without any prior contact.

**Adhocracy.** A type of management who is unwilling to do planning and only responds to immediate problems.

**Adhocratic management.** A management style that concentrates only on individual problems instead of overall organisation's growth.

**Adjourning stage.** The last stage of group development in case of temporary groups which is characterized by attention towards wrapping up activities. The group prepares for its disbandment. At this moment, some group members may be in a celebrating mood over group's achievements and others may be sad and depressed over the loss of friendships gained during group's life or duration.

**Adjournment.** The temporary stoppage of the negotiation process. This is usually done in order to allow time to two parties to think.

**Adjudication.** 1. The judgment of a court. 2. A dispute prevention and settlement machinery set up under Industrial Disputes Act, 1948* comprising of labour court*, industrial tribunal* and national tribunal*.

**Administration.** A top-level thinking function in an organisation which is concerned with the determination of major policies and objectives. Used largely in government departments, educational institutions, public sectors, etc. Administrative decisions are influenced basically by public opinion and other outside forces.

**Administration and management.** The two terms used interchangeably as both involve the same principles and functions. Somehow, the term management has become more famous in business organisations where economic performance is of main importance. And the term administration is more preferred in government departments, educational institutes, etc. *See administration, management.*

**Administrative management theory.** An approach to management that emphasizes the significance of formal structure and the hierarchy of an organisation. This is based on contributions made by Henry Fayol (1930) and Max Weber (1922).

**Administrative science.** A systematic study of administration*, as a field, in all its aspects. This includes both the business administration and public administration.

**Administrator.** In business management, an individual who controls or co-ordinates or directs or leads the activities of all of his subordinates.

**Adolescent.** A person who has completed his 15th year of age but has not completed his 18th year.

**Adult.** A person who has completed his 18th year of age.

**Advance.** Payment made earlier i.e. money given before the date when it was due. For example, in case of need, employees take their salary in advance from their employer on request basis.

**Adventure learning.** A training program that focuses on development of teamwork and leadership skills with the help of structured outdoor activities. For example, development of skills relating to group effectiveness like conflict management, risk taking and problem-solving.

**Adverse impact.** The overall impact of employment practices or policies that results in significantly higher percentage of members of minorities and other protected classes being rejected for employment, promotion, etc. This is also known as **disparate impact**. In other words, it is a discrimination which occurs when the same standard is applicable to all applicants/employees, but that standard affects a protected group more adversely (negatively).

**Adverse selection.** A problem with flexible benefit program in which only the higher-risk employees choose and use certain benefits. For example, most of the insurance schemes are based on a group rate, in case insufficient number of employees select an insurance option then the employer may face the problem of higher rate.

**Advertisement.** A form of public announcement. For example, during the recruitment process, a company gives advertisement in media regarding the vacancies in the company.

**Advertiser.** An organisation or an individual on whose behalf an advertisement was given in the media and who ultimately pays bill of advertisement.

**Advertising.** To make publicly known by the use of media like print media (newspaper, journals, magazines) or through TV, radio, internet, etc.

**Advertising agency.** An organisation which prepares and places the advertisement for others. An organisation which acts like an agent for placing the advertisement in media and charging the fees for it. The advertising agency is usually an expert body.

**Advisory committee.** A committee constituted in order to provide advise on specific matters. For example, advisory committee formed for fixation and revision of minimum wages under Minimum Wages Act, 1948.*

**Affective component of an attitude.** One of the three main components of the attitudes an individual have which refers to feeling or emotional segment of an attitude.

**Affidavit.** A declaration in the form of a written statement, sworn on oath to be true. If a person makes a false statement in an affidavit then it is a criminal offence.

**Affiliation need.** The desire or the need to 'belong' to a group. It is a motivational factor.

**Affiliative group.** Any reference group to which a person belongs like school, team, church, family, etc.

**Affinity card.** A credit card which is issued to the members of an affinity group. For example, members of campus, club, occupation, etc.

**Affirmative action.** A strategy designed to attain the goal of fair employment by recommending employers to hire certain groups of people who were discriminated against in the past.

**Affirmative action plan (AAP).** A formal document that an employer must compile annually for submission to the enforcement agencies. Under U.S. law, the federal, state and local regulations require employers to compile AAP* in order to report on the composition of their employees. The intention of the law is to force the employers to address the areas of potential discrimination (for example, women and minorities, etc.).

**Agency shop.** A union security form in which the employees who are not the members of the union must still pay the union dues on the assumption that the union efforts benefit all the employees.

**Agenda.** The detailed list of the items to be dealt with in a meeting. The agenda is sent to all the persons invited to attend the meeting.

**Agent.** A person (for example, a manager) who is expected to act on the behalf of a principal (for example, the owner of the firm).

**Agreeableness.** A personality dimension which describes an individual as cooperative, trusting and good-natured.

**Agreed procedure.** A procedure which is agreed to be followed while attempting to solve any grievance between trade union and management before resorting to a strike or a lockout. In case, a strike or a lockout is called first without going through the agreed procedure then it is considered to be an unconstitutional strike or a lockout.

**AGV.** Abbreviation for automated guided vehicle.*

**Aiming.** It is a type of psychomotor skill. It is a person's ability to perform accurately and quickly/swiftly a sequence of movements which demands eye-hand co-ordination.

**AITUC.** Abbreviation for All India Trade Union Congress, formed in 1920.

**All-in rate.** A wage rate which includes several extras like bonus in addition to the basic time rate payment.

**Allocable surplus.** The workers' share in the available surplus*.

**Alternate.** An individual appointed to act as a substitute for another individual in performing certain duties, whenever the other individual is not available.

**Alternate director.** An individual who can act, for a time being, on the behalf of a director of company in his absence.

**Alternate form method.** A method of determining reliability of a test in which on first time, a test is given and for the second time, an alternate/similar form of the test is administered. Also known as **parallel or equivalent form method.** However, it is difficult and costly to develop two separate and equivalent tests.

**Alternate standard.** A term used for alternate standard time when an alternative method is used.

**Alternating day and night.** An arrangement, when a company works on a two-shift basis, then one group of employees work for a period (like a week, fortnight or a month) on a day shift then for the same period on a night shift.

**Alternating shift.** When a company operates on a shift basis, then workers are shifted/changed periodically to a different shift (often weekly or fortnightly or monthly).

**Alternation ranking method.** A performance appraisal method in which employees are ranked from best to worst on a trait or traits, choosing highest then lowest until all the employees are ranked.

**Alternative dispute resolution.** A grievance handling procedure that provides for binding arbitration as the last stage. Also known as **ADR program**. Under this program, usually new recruits are required to sign this agreement as a condition of employment and the present employees are required to sign this agreement prior to transfer or promotion.

**Alternative staffing arrangements.** Hiring temporary or contract employees to supplement the permanent workforce. Use of contingent or temporary or part-time or just-in-time workers is growing and widespread.

**Amalgamation.** The combination of two or more parties or organisations into a major party or organisation. According to the Trade Unions Act, 1926*, any 2 or more registered trade unions may become amalgamated only when votes of at least one-half of the members of each trade union entitled to vote are recorded, and that at least 60 per cent of the votes recorded are in favour of the proposal of amalgamation.

**Amendment.** An improvement or minor alteration in the existing law or system.

**Americans with disabilities act (ADA).** Enacted in 1990, this U.S. act prohibits the discrimination of individuals with disabilities at the workplace.

**Analysis.** Separation or breakdown of total figure into its components.

**Analysis of variance (ANOVA).** A statistical technique designed especially to test whether the means of more than two quantitative populations are equal. It is developed by R.A. Fisher in 1920's.

**Analytic approach.** An approach to assess the effectiveness of human resource management* (HRM*) practices. This is done by either determining the effect of newly introduced program or practice, or by estimating the financial costs and benefits from the HRM* practice or program.

**Analytical estimating.** A work measurement technique in which the time needed to carry out the elements of a job is estimated.

**Annual bonus.** A short-term incentive designed to encourage short-term performance of executives and managers, usually tied to the organisation's profitability. For awarding short-term incentives, generally three basic issues are considered; these are fund size, eligibility and individual awards.

**Annual hours work plan.** A work-related plan in which employees agreed to work for a certain number of hours per year instead of per week or month. This is a contractual arrangement between an employer and his employees.

**Annual plan.** An organisation's short-term plan which is concerned about the organisation's present situation, its future strategy, objectives and goals, budget for the coming year and also the action and central program.

**Annuitant.** An individual who receives an annuity*.

**Annuity.** A fixed amount paid to an individual every year. This is paid as a result of a contract between that individual and an insurance company, the individual pays a premium to the insurance company, generally in one lump sum and in return gets periodic payments for a certain period for the rest of his life.

**Annuity certain.** An annuity* in which an insurance company make continuous payments for a specified period irrespective of the life or death of the individual covered under the policy.

**ANOVA.** Abbreviation for Analysis of Variance*.

**Anticipatory socialization.** A part of organizational socialization process that occurs before a person joins the organization. In this, individuals expectations about the job, firm, working conditions and interpersonal relationships are developed by company representatives during the recruitment and selection.

**Appellant.** An individual or an organisation who files an appeal in the higher court. The party which resists that appeal is known as respondent.

**Applicant pool.** All the persons who are actually evaluated for the selection.

**Applicant population.** A subset of the total labour force population which is available for selection depending upon the recruitment approach adopted. For example, a firm might limit its recruitment for software engineers to only IIT graduates.

**Application form.** A form that provides information regarding the applicant's education, skills and prior work experience. Usually, this is the first step in the selection process.

**Appraisal.** Assessment of an employee's performance. *See performance appraisal.*

**Appraisal interview.** An interview, conducted after the performance appraisal, in which the supervisor and the subordinate review the outcome of the appraisal and prepare plans to reinforce strengths and remedy weaknesses.

**Appraisal politics.** A situation when evaluators intentionally distort a rating in order to attain their personal or organizational goal.

**Apprentice.** A person learning a craft or trade and bound to an employer under a legal agreement.

**Apprenticeship.** A program by which people/prospective employees become skilled employees through a combination of on-the-job training and classroom instructions.

**Apprenticeship training.** A training program which aims at providing the essential background, practical knowledge, experience to the employee. Very useful for learning a particular trade and craft. This type of training combines the classroom instructions, demonstrations and on-the-job training.

**Appropriate government.** In respect of all the establishments under the control of the central government or a railway administration or a major port or a mine or oilfield it is the central government. And in all the other cases, it means the state government.

**Approve.** To give sanction officially.

**Aptitude.** The natural ability or readiness of an employee to learn specific skills.

**Aptitude test.** A test of an individual's ability to learn a particular task.

**Arbitration.** A process of settling a dispute by an arbitrator or arbitrators rather than by a court. Usually this is the last stage in a grievance handling procedure. The decision of the arbitrator or arbitrators is binding on both the parties.

**Arbitrator.** An independent (neutral or impartial) person chosen from outside the organisation to settle a dispute.

**Area sampling.** A type of probability sampling in which the stratified sample is made on the basis of geography (i.e., area-wise like city, district, village, etc.).

**Arithmetic mean.** An average, its value is obtained by adding together all items and by dividing this total by the number of items.

**Armed truce.** A union-management relation in which each party views the other party as antagonistic but tries to avoid head on conflict. The collective bargaining obligations and contract provisions are very strictly interpreted.

**Assertiveness training.** A training program which is designed to maximize the employees potential, raise their self-esteem, develop their abilities so that they can rightly, confidently and convincingly express themselves and transform their ideas into actions.

**Assessment.** 1. To identify the ability of candidates during the recruitment and selection. 2. A collection of all information about the employees and providing them feedback regarding their behaviour, communication skills and personality types.

**Assessment center.** A place where the candidates, usually managers, are required to perform a set of simulated exercises or tasks. And the observers rate performance based on these simulated exercises/tasks and make inferences about each candidate's managerial skills.

**Associate union membership.** A form of union membership in which the union collects dues in exchange of services like health and life insurance, etc. but does not provide representation in collective bargaining*.

**Assured.** An insured person or a beneficiary of an insurance policy.

**At risk variable pay plan.** A pay plan that put some part or portion of the employee's pay at risk, subject to the organisation's meeting its financial goals. When the employees reach or exceed their goals, then they earn incentives otherwise they forgo some of the salary they would normally have earned.

**ATM.** Abbreviation for Automated Teller Machine*. Also famous for All Time Money.

**Attainment test.** A type of psychological test which measures knowledge in a specific area or attainment in a specific skill. Also known as achievement test.

**Attendance bonus.** In addition to normal wages, bonus given to those employees who are regular or not absent from their work.

**Attest.** To legalize some document by having the signatures on them of a third party, it means they have been attested.

**Attitude.** A person's way of thinking and evaluating someone or something. A person's positive or negative thinking about an object (a product or service). It determines whether a person likes or dislikes someone or something and so that he behaves accordingly.

**Attitude awareness program.** A program that focus on providing employees an awareness regarding differences in cultural and ethnic backgrounds, physical characteristics (for example, disabilities) and personal characteristics which influence behaviour toward other persons. This program helps to avoid employees negative stereotypes when they interact with employees of different backgrounds.

**Attitude discrepant behaviour.** A person's behaviour which is inconsistent or not accordingly with his usual attitudes. This type of behaviour is usually motivated by a desire to attain a specific goal or to make a good impression on others.

**Attitude survey.** A survey which is used to collect information about employees' beliefs, feelings and views about their jobs, supervisors, co-workers and organizational policies and practices. This survey is significant in reducing labour turnover and thus, increase employee retention. The attitude surveys may be developed by academicians.

**Attitudinal structuring.** The part of labour-management negotiation process which refers to the level of trust and relationship between the two parties. For example, poor relationship and little level of trust between the negotiators makes it difficult for them to engage in integrative bargaining.

**Attribution theory.** A theory which states that we judges people differently depending on what meaning we attribute to a given behaviour.

**Attrition.** A policy that is designed to reduce or trim the organization's workforce by not refilling the job vacancies that are created by turnover. This is the least disruptive way to cut the labour costs.

**Attrition rate.** The ratio of the employees who leave the organization to the total number of employees in a year.

**Audioconferencing.** The use of telephone in order to conduct a conference that allows several members sitting at different places to participate in the business meeting.

**Audio response device.** A device which when connected to a computer produces human speech.

**Audiovisual instructions/techniques.** The use of slides, overheads video and multimedia instruments in order to show the trainees real-life experiences and examples of job conditions. These are most famous instructional methods these days. These are used to enhance customer-service skills, communication skills, etc.

**Audit approach.** An approach to evaluate the effectiveness of human resource management* (HRM*) practices. It focuses on reviewing the various outcomes of the HRM* functional areas such as customer satisfaction and key indicators (for example, absenteeism, turnover rate, etc.).

**Authority.** The right to take decisions, to issue orders and to get the decisions carried out. Authority can be delegated.

**Autocratic control.** A tight personal control of an organisation by its manager or chairman.

**Automated answer.** A set answer or response to a routine query which can be easily answered by a computer.

**Automated guided vehicle (AGV).** The self-propelled vehicle used in companies to carry materials without any human intervention. Very useful to transport hazardous chemicals in manufacturing plants.

**Automated teller machine (ATM).** A computerized machine usually located in a separate cabin (outside or away from bank premises) which enables the bank customers to withdraw cash (or do other banking related operations) from their accounts 24 hours in a day.

**Automation.** The replacement of manual system by automatically driven equipment and machinery.

**Autonomous work team.** A team which is allocated an overall task (whole and meaningful piece of work) to do. Team is responsible for the planning, execution and control of the work processes. Also known as self-managing team.

**Autonomy.** The extent of individual freedom at the workplace and in the work scheduling.

**Autorespond e-mail.** A computerized system that enables to answer automatically a query by e-mail without any human intervention.

**Availability analysis.** An analysis which identify the number of the protected class members available for the work in the suitable labour markets in the given jobs.

**Availability heuristic.** The tendency of individual to base their judgments on the information which is readily available to them. For example, media gives more attention to air accidents rather than car accidents, as a result people take flying is more dangerous rather than car driving.

**Available surplus.** In respect of any accounting year, it is the gross profit made by an organisation after making some required deductions.

**AVC.** Abbreviation for Additional Voluntary Contribution*.

**Avoidable costs.** The costs which are not incurred if an alternative decision is taken. For example, if a particular project is not taken up, then the labour and material costs may not be incurred.

**Award.** 1. An interim or final determination of any industrial dispute by labour court,* industrial tribunal* or national tribunal*. It is a binding on the concerned parties until and unless an appeal is preferred. 2. An individual based pay plan that provides one-time reward. Usually given in the form of a tangible prize like a foreign trip for two persons, a paid vocation, etc.

# B

**Backdate.** To compile a document in the earlier date rather than today's so that it becomes active from the earlier date.

**Backlog.** The accumulation of all uncompleted tasks or work.

**Balance of payments.** The difference between the payment a nation makes to the other nations and those it receives over a certain period of time.

**Balance of trade.** The relationship between the values of a country's exports and imports when exports exceed imports then trade surplus exists. When imports exceeds exports then trade deficit exists.

**Balance sheet approach.** An approach to international compensation that is designed to equalize the cost differences between the foreign assignments and those in the home country. It maintains the home country living standard plus a financial inducement to make the total package attractive. This links the basic salary for parent country nationals* (PCNs) and third country nationals* (TCNs) to the salary structure of the relevant home country.

**Balanced scorecard.** A measure of company performance that indicates managers to look at their firm from the angles of internal and external customers, shareholders and employees.

**Baldridge award.** *See Malcolm Baldridge National Quality Award (MBNQA).*

**Bandh.** A form of industrial dispute which means closed or locked. It conveys the idea that everything is to be closed or blocked. Giving call for and holding of bandh is unconstitutional as it violates the fundamental rights guaranteed to workers.

**Bar chart/diagram.** A chart or a diagram which presents the statistical data in the form of rectangles (or bars) of various heights.

**Bargaining.** Discussions on the terms of an agreement.

**Bargaining structure.** The basic rules established in an organisation in order to facilitate the bargaining between the trade unions and management.

**Bargaining unit.** A group of employees the trade union will be authorized to represent during bargaining.

**BARS.** Abbreviation for Behaviourally Anchored Rating Scale*.

**Base compensation.** The fixed pay an employee receives on a regular basis. Usually, it is the first and largest element of the total compensation package.

**Base pay.** The basic compensation an employee receives.

**Base period.** A year or a span of years which are used as a reference point and to which the present data is compared. This is done for business research purposes.

**Basic research.** The research which aims at adding more to knowledge rather than solving a particular problem.

**Basic skills.** The reading, writing and communication skills in a person.

**Basic workweek.** The number of hours in a normal workweek.

**Battery.** A collection of tests that serves a similar purpose or they have to be administered one after the another at a single session.

**Beadaux plan.** An individual incentive system in which each minute of the allowed time is called a beadaux point or 'B' in short. In one hour, there are 60 Bs. Each job in the firm has a standard number of Bs and the hourly rate is also determined. In addition to hourly rate, an employee also receives a bonus calculated at 75 per cent of the points earned in excess of 60 per hour, multiplied by one-sixtieth of the worker's hourly rate.

**Behaviour-based programs.** A program that concentrate on changing the individual behaviours and company policies that hinder/restrain employee's personal growth and productivity.

**Behaviour-based safety.** An accident prevention program that consists of identifying employee behaviours which contribute towards accidents and then provide training to employees to avoid these behaviours.

**Behaviour expectation scales (BES).** An appraisal scale in which the anchors are illustrations that help the evaluator to define the behaviour of the employee as superior, average or below average.

**Behaviour modeling.** Off-the-job training and development technique. In this, firstly the trainees are shown the right or model way of doing something, then let the trainees practice themselves that role in a simulated environment and finally provide them feedback as well as praise on their performance by their supervisor. Basically, the procedure involves: modeling (trainees watching films showing models behaving effectively), role playing (trainees practice and rehearse the effective behaviours), social reinforcement (praise and constructive feedback based on their performance) and transfer of training (encouraging trainees to apply their new skills on their jobs).

**Behaviour observation scale (BOS).** An appraisal scale in which the evaluators rate the subordinate on the basis of frequency of the critical incidents. The evaluators note down the frequency of critical employee behaviours as they are observed to occur in a given period of time and rate subordinates according to that.

**Behavioural appraisal instrument.** An appraisal instrument that asks managers to assess an employee by behaviours (for example, punctuality, works well with coworkers, etc).

**Behavioural component of an attitude.** A person's intention to behave in a particular or certain way (positive manner or in a negative manner) toward something or someone. The person's intention is based on his attitude toward that object or person.

**Behavioural engineering.** A concept that people behave in direct relation to what they believe will be the consequences of their acts. Also known as Skinnerian psychology, applied behavioural analysis and behavioural technology.

**Behavioural interviews.** A series of job-related questions that ask interviewees to describe how they reached to the actual situations in the past (on the other hand, situational interviews ask interviewees to describe how they would react to a hypothetical situation today or tomorrow).

**Behavioural rating approach.** An approach that assesses an employee's behaviours instead of other characteristics for example, behaviourally anchored rating scale*, behaviour expectation scales* and behaviour observation scales*.

**Behavioural research.** The research into the human behaviour, either individually or in groups.

**Behavioural theories of leadership.** The theories that focus on certain specific or critical behaviours in order to differentiate the leaders from non-leaders.

**Behaviourally anchored rating scale (BARS).** A performance appraisal technique that attempts to evaluate job performance in terms of critical behaviours that are important to success or failure on the job. The BARS are produced by merging critical incident method with the graphic rating concept. Basically, the evaluators rate the critical employee behaviour.

**Belief.** A person's thought or understanding about a thing or occurrence.

**Benchmark job.** A job that is similar or comparable content-wise across organisation and used to anchor the pay scales. Around a benchmark job, other jobs are arranged according to their relative work.

**Benchmarking.** Identification of industry's best practices with the aim of using them as a guide (or reference point) in order to improve an organisation's own practices.

**Benefits.** An important part of an employee's compensation that includes indirect financial and non-financial payments the employees receives for continuing their employment with the organisation. For example, pensions, child care facilities/crèches, health and life insurance, pay for time not worked, etc.

**Benefits in kind.** The benefits apart from the cash arising from an employment.

**Benefits mix.** The total package of benefits that an organisation offers to its employees.

**Benefits needs analysis.** A detailed analysis of all aspects of benefits.

**Bereavement pay.** The pay given to an employee when he was on leave due to the death of his close relative.

**Bernenter personality inventory.** A test designed to assess a candidate's personality. It measures person's sociability, self-sufficiency, introversion, extroversion, self-confidence, neurotic tendency and locus of control.

**BES.** Abbreviation for Behaviour Expectation Scales*.

**BFOQ.** Abbreviation for Bona fide Occupational Qualification*.

**Bias.** In performance appraisal, this is the tendency to allow the individual differences like race, age and sex to affect the ratings of employees.

**Bilateral contract.** A contract between the two parties. The two parties agree for some mutual obligations. Most of the contracts are bilateral in nature. However, from economic and political perspectives, multilateral contracts (between more than 2 parties) are more prevalent now.

**Biographical characteristics.** The employees personal characteristics like age, martial status, gender, etc.

**Black leg.** An employee who works when his fellow employees are on strike i.e., who does not support the union decision or action. A worker who refuses to join a union.

**Blank application.** An application form given to the candidates for filling their facts, i.e., educational qualification, work experience, etc.

**Blanket agreement.** The collective agreement which results from the industry wide or national bargaining.

**Blind ad.** An advertisement which shows no identification of the organisation. The respondents are asked to respond/reply to a post box number or to a consulting company hired by the organisation.

**Blocked need satisfaction.** A situation when the satisfaction of a particular need is blocked, then a reduction in the strength of the need may result.

**Blue-collar worker.** A worker working in manufacturing areas with low-pay jobs, mostly manual labourers. The blue collar refers to the blue dress usually worn by manual workers in the factories.

**Board of conciliation.** An industrial dispute settlement machinery set up under Industrial Dispute Act, 1947*. According to this act, the central and state government may constitute a board of conciliation for promoting the settlement of a dispute. The board shall submit the full report to appropriate government* (regarding the details of conciliation proceedings and steps taken by the board) within 2 months of the date on which the dispute was referred to it.

**Board representative.** A form of workers participation in management* (WPM*) in which workers representative participate in the organisation's board of directors and represent workers interest.

**Bona fide occupational qualification (BFOQ).** Under American Civil Rights Act 1964, it is a characteristic which must be present in all employees for a specific job. This is a basic defense that an employer can use. According to it, it should not be an unlawful employment practice for an employer to hire an employee on the basis of race, religion, sex or national origin when it is reasonably essential to the organisation's normal operation.

**Bonus.** A one-time (usually once a year) financial incentive given to employee and that does not raise the employee's basic pay permanently.

**Bonus formula.** A formula which determines the total funds available for bonus payments in a given year. The individual bonus payments are given from this total pool of funds.

**BOS.** Abbreviation for Behaviour Observation Scales*.

**Bottom up approach.** An approach to decision-making in which people at lower level of organizational hierarchy are consulted. This is just opposite to top-down approach in which decision and instructions flow from top to bottom.

**Boundaryless organisation.** An organisation structure in which an organisation forms relationships with suppliers, customers and even with competitors, in order to pool the resources for mutual benefit or to promote cooperation in a volatile business environment. For example, forming joint ventures that allows organisations to share intellectual property rights, skilled workforce, limited financial resources, distribution networks, etc.

**Bounded rationality.** As a result of limited capacity of the human mind for formulating and solving complex problems, people make decisions by making simplified models that extract the essential features from the problems without capturing all their complexity.

**Boycott.** An appeal to the workers to voluntary withdraw the co-operation. It is persuasive in nature but negative in approach. The aim is to disrupt the routine/normal functioning of the firm.

**BPR**. Abbreviation for Business Process Reengineering*.

**Brain drain.** The loss of well-qualified and highly talented personnel to startup ventures, competitors and foreign nations.

**Brainstorming.** A creativity training technique that provide opportunity to the participants to express their ideas openly, without any fear of judgment or rejection. Every idea is thoroughly discussed and evaluated even if it is irrelevant one. It attempts to help people solve problems in new way.

**Branch.** A geographically separated/ detached unit of an organisation but which is still an integral part of the organisation.

**Breakaway union.** A new trade union formed by a group or section of dissident (disagreeing) members who have withdrawn from an existing trade union.

**Broadbanding.** Combining salary grades into few wide bands or levels, each of which consists of a relatively wide range of jobs and salary levels.

**Brown-spearman formula.** A method of validating an intelligent test especially when the length of the test has been increased and the validity of this extended test needed to be checked.

**Brownfield development.** An industrial or housing development within a already existing urban area.

**Budget.** A plan of an organisation's anticipated revenue and proposed expenditure in the next financial year.

**Bumper strike.** An earlier type of strike in which the striking workers are directly financially supported by the similar workers in other factories.

**Bumping/layoff* procedures**. The detailed procedures, prepared by employers who face frequent business slowdowns and layoffs, that determines who will be laid off when no work is available. Usually, the procedure provides employees to use their seniority in order to remain on the job.

**Bureaucracy.** A term applied to a system of government, the control of which is so completely in the hands of officials that most of the times their power endangers the liberties of the ordinary citizens.

**Bureaucratic management.** A style of management which is based on the principles of bureaucracy i.e., which concentrates on the hierarchical authority, procedures, rules and regulation.

**Bureaupathology.** The clear indications of aggravated bureaucratic behaviour like total reliance on rules and regulations, resistance to change, lack of ability to handle an unpredictable situation, etc. Also known as **red-tape syndrome**.

**Bureausis.** A person's strong reaction against the bureaucratic behaviour. The person refuses to follow the rules and regulations blindly.

**Burnout.** A work-related situation in which an individual is emotionally exhausted and he loses interest in his work. The efficiency of the employee declines and he becomes incapable of making decisions.

**Business.** The activities related with manufacturing goods and providing services, buying and selling goods in order to make profit.

**Business administration.** An art and a branch of science which deals with conducting business with minimum cost and optimum utilization of all resources.

**Business agent.** A full-time trade union official who runs the union office and assists the other union members.

**Business analysis.** An analysis or review of the company's current performance. For example, SWOT analysis.

**Business necessity.** An employer's defense created by the courts. It just need proving that there is an overriding legitimate business purposes for the discriminatory practice.

**Business plan.** A comprehensive plan of the objectives and goals of a business over a certain stated period like 3, 5 or 10 years.

**Business process reengineering (BPR).** A radical redesign of business processes to achieve dramatic improvements in quality, speed, service and cost. The term reengineering was coined by Michael Hammer and James Champy in their book 'Reengineering the Corporation'.

**Business unionism.** A form of unionism which is essentially trade-conscious rather than class-conscious. It focuses on improving workers' economic well-being by laying stress on improvement in wages, working conditions and working hours.

**Business unit strategy.** Formulation and implementation of strategies by an organisation which is relatively autonomous even if it is a part of a bigger organisation.

**Buzz group.** A type of brainstorming group which is used in management problem-solving.

**Bye turnman.** An individual employed in casual labour.

# C

**CAD.** Abbreviation for Computer-Aided Design.*

**Cafeteria system.** A benefit program in which employers allow their employees to select the benefits they prefer the most from a menu of choices. This is based on the concept that employees have diverse needs which requires different benefits packages. Also known as flexible benefit program.

**Call center.** A center or an office which mainly handles a large number of outgoing or incoming phone calls.

**CAM.** Abbreviation for Computer-Aided Manufacturing.*

**Candidate-order error.** An error that occurs during interviewing the candidates, which means the order in which the interviewer see the applicants affects how he rate them. For example, after evaluating numerous unfavourable candidates, the interviewer might evaluate 'just average' candidate more favourably. Also known as **contrast error.**

**CAPI.** Abbreviation for Computer-Aided Personal Interview*.

**Card steward.** A trade union official who is responsible for collecting the trade union dues.

**Career.** A series of positions a person occupies or progresses throughout his life.

**Career management system.** A system that identifies and meet employee's development needs. This is significant in order to motivate and retain the employees especially the good performers. Also known as **career development planning system.**

**Career path.** A path which shows the various stages/steps in a possible career and a schedule for accomplishing them. It indicates the possible directions and career-related opportunities available within the company.

**Career planning and development.** A deliberate, ongoing and formalized process that focuses on developing more capable and enriched employees.

**Career resource center.** A center that collects material like texts, reports, tapes and work books. Usually, this resource center is maintained by human resource department. It helps the individuals to identify for themselves their own strengths and weaknesses, training and development opportunities and the various career options.

**Career support.** The protection, sponsorship, coaching, guiding, exposure and providing challenging assignments. This is a part of employee development program.

**Case study method.** A development method in which a written description of an actual business situation is presented to the trainees for diagnose. Trainees are asked to study the case in detail and determine what are the problems, analyse causes, develop alternative solutions, choose the best one and then implement it.

**Cash balance pension plan.** An employee benefit (retirement) plan in which the employer, contributes a percentage of the employees' present salary to the employees pension plans each year and employees earn interest at a predetermined rate on that amount.

**Cash labour.** The workers who are not employed on regular basis but only when work is available.

**CASI.** Abbreviation for Computer-Aided Self-Interview Test*.

**Casual.** A worker or a job which is not regular or permanent i.e., which is part-time, temporary or occasional in nature. Casual workers do not have any share in job-related benefits like pension, gratuity and provident fund.

**Casual work.** Irregular work in the organisation.

**CATI.** Abbreviation for Computer Assisted Telephone Interviewing*.

**Causal research.** A research technique in which it is determined that whether a change in one variable has caused some observed change in other variable or not.

**CBT.** Abbreviation for Computer Based Training*.

**Census survey.** A complete enumeration survey method in which data are collected for each and every unit (for example, an individual, field, household, factory, shop, etc.) of the population or mass or universe.

**Central tendency error.** An error that occurs during performance appraisal in which all the employees are rated incorrectly near the average or in the mid dle of the rating scale.

**Centralization.** Concentration of the decision-making authority on the top level of the organisation structure.

**Certificate.** A written document which provides an evidence of a fact.

**Certificate of fitness.** Under Factories Act, 1948*, a certificate granted to a young person* by a certifying surgeon* after examining him and ascertaining his fitness for work in a factory. This certificate entitles a young person to work as a child or adult in a factory.

**Certifying surgeon.** A qualified medical practitioner appointed by the state government for specified local limits or factories. His duties includes the examination and certification of young persons, the examination of persons engaged in factories in dangerous occupations or processes and exercising medical supervision as may be prescribed for any factory*.

**Chairperson.** The presiding officer of a committee, meeting or an organization. Also known as **chairman**, or **chairwomen** or even sometimes simply **chair**.

**Change agent.** A person or a group (for example, an outside management consultant) who brings a change in the existing practices of an organisation.

**Channel richness.** The amount of information that can be transmitted during a communication episode, i.e., which offers multiple information hints/

cues (like words, gestures, postures, facial expressions).

**Charge head.** A worker who performs almost same work as others do in the group but he is given some supervisory duties also.

**Charisma.** A person's capability to influence or persuade successfully other people.

**Charismatic management.** A style of management which is based on the authority accepted by the members because of charisma (personal qualities) of the manager or supervisor in an organisation.

**Checking references.** A step/stage while hiring a candidate in which the references provided by the applicant are checked or contacted in order to know the applicant's past employment record (regarding his character and reputation).

**Checklist.** A performance appraisal instrument which consists of a list of statements or words to be checked by the evaluators. The evaluators will tick the statements that are most representative of the characteristics of performance of the employees. For example, (i) attendance satisfactory (yes/no), (ii) obey order (yes/no), (iii) cooperative and helpful (yes/no), etc.

**Check off system.** A union contract provision or a practice in which the employer deduct employees' union dues from their paycheck and gives the lump sum amount to the union.

**Chief executive.** A person who usually has the authority over all the other members in the organisation.

**Child.** A person who has not completed his 15th year of age.

**Child labour.** The employment of children who are below 14th year of age.

**Chronic unemployment.** A long-term unemployment which lasts from six months or longer. It may be caused by technological changes, overall slowdown in the economy or structural changes in the economy.

**Chunk.** A fraction of population being investigated which is selected by convenience and not by either probability* or by judgment.

**Circular.** A notice in an organisation either given by hand or distributed by post to large number of members.

**Citation.** In U.S., under Occupational Safety and Health Act (OSHA), 1970, this refers to the summons (order to appear before a magistrate or judge at a particular date, time and place) informing the employers and employees regarding the violations of the standards and regulations at the workplace.

**Civilian labour force.** The total working population of a country. This includes all the persons of 14 years of age or above who are either gainfully employed or are unemployed but they are seeking a job.

**Class conflict.** The conflict between the working class (who are interested in having high wages) and the employing class (who are interested in giving low wages).

**Classes.** The grouping of the jobs based on a set of rules for each class or group like skill, judgment, physical effort, mental effort, etc. required. Usually, classes include similar jobs.

**Classical conditioning theory.** A learning theory that explains a type of conditioning in which a person responds to some stimulus that generally would not produce that response. It grews out of the experiments conducted to teach the dogs to salivate in response to the ringing bell.

**Classical school of management.** *See administrative management theory.*

**Clear days.** The full days in a contract, without including the starting or last day of the contract.

**Clerical work improvement program.** A technique of work measurement in offices which is based on the predetermined time and motion systems.

**Client-server architecture.** A computer design which provide a method to consolidate data and the applications into a single system (i.e. the client). This data can be accessed by multiple users.

**Closed-ended questions.** The questions on a questionnaire which ask the respondents to choose from the given answers.

**Closed shop.** A union security provision that requires a person must be a member of the union at the time of his employment and continue to do so in order to retain his job. In other words, a firm can hire only union members.

**Closure.** The permanent closing down of a place of employment or a part thereof.

**Cluster.** A group of people or households which have several common characteristics in them.

**Cluster sampling.** A type of probability sampling* in which the random selection is made of primary, intermediate and final units from a given population. In this, sampling process is carried out at several stages. First of all, suitable method like simple random sampling*, then a sample* of the second stage units is selected from each of the selected first stage units by suitable method (which may be same or different from the earlier method). For example, first stage may be a state, then districts is second stage, then third stage be villages. Also called as **multi-stage sampling.**

**Coach.** A trainer or an expert (for example, a manager) who help the employees in learning new skills, motivate them, provide reinforcement and feedback.

**Coaching.** An on-the-job training method in which a superior or supervisor plays the role of a guide and instructor of the trainees. He provide guidance, instructions and demonstrations to the trainees.

**Code of conduct.** A set of guidelines regarding the ethical principles and desirable behaviour of a professional organisation.

**Code of discipline.** A way of promoting industrial peace by securing settlement of disputes and grievances by negotiation*, conciliation* and voluntary arbitration*. It is a government induced self-imposed and mutually agreed voluntary principle of discipline and relations between the employer and employees. It came into force from June 1, 1958. It aims at avoidance of work stoppages, facilitate the free growth of trade unions and maintain discipline in industry*.

**Codetermination.** The workers' representation on the organisations' board of directors. This is based on the concept that labour and capital should be the partners in the organisation.

**Coding.** A process of assigning numerals or other symbols to the answers obtained in a research study so that the responses can be put into a limited number of classes or categories. It is essential for efficient analysis as several replies are reduced to a number of classes which contain the critical information needed for analysis.

**Coercion.** The use of threat, force or power to get the people to do something which they otherwise will not.

**Cognition.** A term used for all psychological processes through which people become aware about the world.

**Cognitive ability.** An individual's reasoning power, thinking, memory, verbal comprehension and mathematical ability. It is significant as it influences the job performance and ability of an individual to learn in a training and development program.

**Cognitive ability tests.** The tests which measure an individual's reasoning ability, memory, verbal and quantitative/ mathematical ability.

**Cognitive component of an attitude.** The belief or opinion segment of an attitude.

**Cognitive dissonance.** Any incompatibility that a person might perceive between 2 or more of his attitudes or between his behaviour and attitudes.

**Cognitive processes.** All those mental processes or activities that involve reasoning like judging and learning.

**Cognitive resource theory.** A theory of leadership which states that the stress unfavourably affects a situation and that the experience and intelligence of a leader can lessen the influence of the stress on him. This theory was developed by Fred Fiedler and Joe Garcia.

**Cohesiveness.** The degree to which all members of a group are attracted to each other and are motivated to stay in group.

**Cohorts.** The persons who as a part of a group held a common attribute. For example, people born before 1947 have experienced the war for independence.

**Coinsurance.** The payments that are made to cover the health care expenses which are divided between the employer's insurance firm and the employee. For example, in a 70/30 insurance plan, the employer's insurance firm would pay 70 per cent of the employee's health care expenses and the rest 30 per cent would be paid by the employee.

**COLA.** Abbreviation for Cost-Of-Living Adjustment*.

**Collective bargaining.** A process in which the representatives of labour union and the management representatives negotiate with each other a labour agreement. The agreement may include issues related with wages, benefits, working hours and other terms and conditions of employment.

**Collusion.** A union-management relation in which both the parties cooperate to the extent of adversely affecting the legitimate interests of employees, other businesses in the industry and the consuming public. This involves convincing to control markets, supplies and prices illegally or unethically.

**Combination strategy.** A business strategy usually followed by large firms in which they expand their business in some areas and cut back (withdraw) in other areas. Expansion in a growing and profitable sector and withdrawal in a loosing sector.

**Command group.** A group determined by the organizational chart, composed of individuals who report directly to a given manager or boss. For example, a head of department and his 10 teachers.

**Commission.** A payment/compensation* made to the employee as a percentage of sales in units or rupees.

**Commitment.** An employee's identification with the organisation and its goals.

**Committee.** A group of people (usually 4 to 8) appointed by the organisation for a specific purpose. For example, works committee set up under Industrial Disputes Act, 1947*. The committee may be a adhoc committee or permanent standing committee.

**Communication.** An exchange of ideas, opinions, facts or emotions to create mutual understanding. It is derived from Latin word 'communis' that means common. It is a systematic and continuous process in which one organisation member shares meaning and understanding with others with the help of messages, attitudes, gestures, actions, feeling, words, letters and symbols.

**Communication apprehension.** A major barrier to effective communication in which the people experience undue tension and anxiety about the oral and written communication or both.

**Communication credibility.** The extent to which the communication of the message is believable or trustworthy.

**Communication network.** A pattern of contacts among the members of an organisation (for example, a circle, chain, wheel, etc.) which determines the rapidity, smoothness and the accuracy with which the messages flow in the organisation. For example, if the network is too long then it may cause delay in the flow of communication.

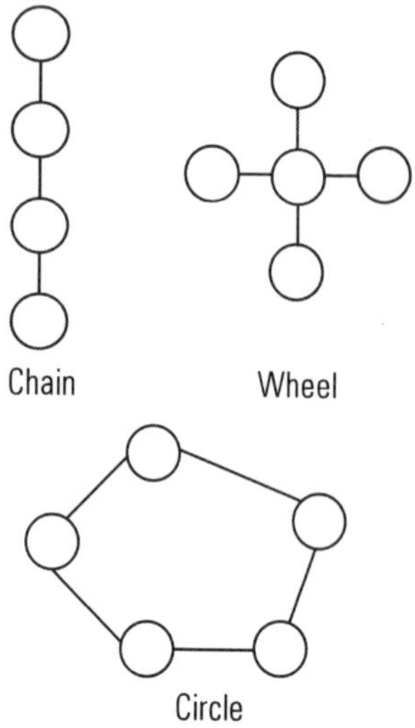


**Communication skill.** The effective communication that creates understanding.

**Communities of practice.** A learning technique in which groups of employees work with each other, learn from each other and develop a common understanding of how to get the work done. This is based on the concept that at workplace, learning occurs as a result of social interactions.

**Compa-ratio.** This measures the degree of consistency of actual pay with the pay policy (intended pay). Numerically, it is calculated as actual pay level divided by the mid-point of the grade.

**Comparability.** In performance measurement, this refers to the degree to which the performance ratings of employees given by the various supervisors/raters in a firm are similar. Specifically, it is concerned with whether during performance appraisal, the supervisors have used the same measurement or not. For example, what one supervisor is considering extraordinary performance, the other one consider it as just average.

**Comparable worth.** A pay concept that emphasizes for comparable pay for the jobs which requires comparable efforts, skills, and responsibility and also have comparable working conditions in spite of difference in the job contents.

**Comparative management.** The study of management in different cultures on a comparative basis. This involves the study of the influence of culture and environment on the management styles.

**Compensable factors.** The work related characteristics which an organization considers most important in measuring the relative value of different jobs. For example, effort, skill, responsibility and working conditions.

**Compensation.** Remuneration of personnel for their contribution to the organisation's goals and objectives. Compensation functions of management includes job evaluation, wage policies and wage systems.

**Compensation committee.** A committee that suggests on the overall pay policies, salaries for the top officers, supplemental compensation like stock options and bonuses and additional perks (perquisites). Usually, it is a subgroup of the board of directors.

**Compensatory damages.** Under America's Civil Rights Act of 1991, these are the fines awarded to a plaintiff (a person who approaches a court with a complaint) in order to compensate for the financial and psychological harm the plaintiff has suffered due to discrimination.

**Compensatory time off (Comp-time).** The time off (hours) given in lieu of the payment for extra time worked.

**Competence authority theory.** The theory which emphasizes that an individual derives authority by his personal competence and charisma.

**Competencies.** The key characteristics (like skill, efficiency, etc.) the presence of which is desired in order to enhance the employee's performance.

**Competency building.** A process of building capabilities of employees in order to enhance their productivity.

**Competency mapping.** Identification of the competencies of all the employees of the company.

**Competent person.** In relation to the Factories Act, 1948* it means a person or an institution recognized as such by the chief inspector for the purpose of carrying out tests, examinations and inspections required to be done in a factory.

**Competitive analysis.** A process of identification of main competitors and assessing their strengths, weaknesses, strategies and objectives.

**Competitive strategy.** A business strategy of a firm which is designed to outdo the actions of its competitors. It is a game plan which involves knowing the likely moves of competitors and then focusing on those moves effectively.

**Competitiveness.** An organisation's ability to gain more and more market share in the industry.

**Complaint.** In an organisation, this is the indicator of employee dissatisfaction or disapproval.

**Compressed workweek.** A type of work schedule redesign in which a full week's work is accomplished in less than five days. The compression changes the number of hours per day per employee, the outcome is longer working hours each day and lesser number of working days per week.

**Computer-aided design (CAD).** Designing of products and manipulating them with the help of computers. It reduces the cost associated with the production of expensive prototypes.

**Computer-aided manufacturing (CAM).** The control of industrial operations or processes with the help of computers. For example, steel manufacturing, oil refining, etc.

**Computer-aided personal interview (CAPI).** A type of interview which is conducted with the use of laptop computers and resulting data is transmitted over the telephone. This method of interview reduces the time and cost of the research process.

**Computer-aided self-interview (CASI).** A types of interview in which the respondent directly interacts with the computer rather than through the interviewer.

**Computer-based training (CBT).** A training method that makes use of computers to show exercises to the participants and they will respond on the system itself. The computer would assess their answers and give result.

**Computerized forecast.** The use of software programs/packages for determining the future manpower needs by projecting sales, volume of production and manpower required.

**Concealed unemployment.** An unemployment which does not appear on the government records or statistics. For example, people doing little productive work and they are not registered as unemployed. Also called as **hidden unemployment**.

**Concentration strategy.** A strategy that emphasize on increasing market share and decreasing costs. This strategy require the organisation to maintain the current skills by providing training program and retain them by providing suitable compensation.

**Conceptual skills.** The ability to visualize the entire picture. It considers a situation in its totality. These skills include the competence to understand a problem in all its aspects and using original thinking in solving the problem.

**Conciliation.** A process in which the representatives of employers and employees are brought together before a third party with a intention of persuading them to reach at an agreement/settlement by mutual discussions. The third party may be an individual or a group of persons.

**Conciliation officer.** An officer appointed under Industrial Disputes Act, 1947* to mediate in and promote the settlement of industrial disputes. His duties includes, hold conciliation proceedings, to investigate the dispute, to send a report and memorandom of settlement to appropriate government*, to send a full report setting forth the steps taken by him in case no settlement is arrived at.

**Conciliation proceeding.** Any proceedings held by a conciliation officer* or board of conciliation* under Industrial Disputes Act, 1947* for the promotion of settlement of any industrial dispute*.

**Concurrent validity.** Concurrent means "existing at the same time", so in this type of validity, job performance measures and the test scores are available at the same time. This is measured by giving a test to the current employees and then correlating their scores with their performance ratings.

**Conditions of employment.** Issues like wages, working hours, benefits, etc. which are usually covered in the employment contract.

**Confidentiality clause.** In the employment contract, this is a clause which contain information an employee would acquire when he joins the organisation and may not passed that information to outsiders.

**Confinement.** Labour resulting in the issue of a living child, or labour after 26 weeks of pregnancy resulting in the issue of a child whether dead or alive.

**Conflict management.** The management of conflicts within an organisation. Mainly there are three philosophies of managing the conflict, (a) **traditionalists.** According to whom conflict is not good and is destructive for an organisation; (b) **behaviourists.** Who view conflict as inevitable and harness it in a positive manner and (c) **interactionists.** Who view conflict as necessary for the survival of an organisation and should be encouraged.

**Conflict of interests.** A situation which arises when an individual acts in two or more different capacities and with different interests. For example, a person is director of two competing companies.

**Conformity.** Adjusting one's behaviour to align with the norms of the group.

**Confravision.** The public video-conferencing with studies in different cities. *See videoconferencing also.*

**Confrontation meetings.** An organisation development intervention that help to clarify and bring problems and misconceptions about intergroup relations into open so that they can be resolved.

**Consequences of training.** The incentives the employees receive for performing better.

**Consideration.** It is one of the dimension of Ohio State Studies which is described as the extent to which an individual is likely to have job relationships which are characterized by mutual trust, respect for the subordinates ideas and regard for their feelings. A leader high in consideration is described as the one who help his employees in their personal problems, treat them equally, is friendly and approachable.

**Constraint.** A factor of production (men, material, machinery, etc.) the shortage of which prevents a company from achieving the optimum levels of performance.

**Construct validity.** Validity that shows/identifies relationship between a psychological trait/abstract characteristic and job performance. Traits includes aggression, creativity, leadership potential, introversion, dominance, etc. A selection procedure is devised in order to measure the presence and degree of the trait which underlies successful job performance.

**Constructive discharge.** A situation in which the employer intentionally make conditions worse and intolerable in order to get an employee to quit or resign. For example, threatening the employee, providing less or tough work, publicly ridiculed by superior, etc.

**Consultative management.** A management style in which subordinates are consulted on various matters and their views are taken.

**Contempt of court.** Any act which means disrespect for law or lawful authority and which hinders the course of justice. It is punishable by fine or imprisonment or with both.

**Content validity.** The validity of a test that is demonstrated by showing that the tests consists of actual/fair sample of the contents of the job. It is measured by nonstatistical methods in order to identify the knowledge, skills and abilities (KSAs) and other characteristics essential for job performance.

**Contextual goals.** The goals that takes into consideration factors which result from the situation in which performance occurs.

**Contingency plan.** A plan formulated to cope with some uncertain situations in future.

**Contingency theory of leadership.** A theory of leadership which focuses on the need for flexibility in dealing with given situations i.e., what may be successful at one time may not be successful at other time.

**Contingent time off.** A job-design practice that allows employees in an organisation to go home when an agreed amount of work, of agreed standard has been finished.

**Contingent workers.** The workers that are hired by the firms in order to deal with temporary (for a time being) rises in the workloads. Hiring of contingent workers is based on the employer's convenience and requirements. These type of workers include part-time/ temporary/outsourced workers.

**Continuous learning.** A learning system in which employees are required to understand the total work system (i.e. relationships among their jobs, their work units and the firm) and they are expected to acquire new knowledge, skills and abilities and then apply them on the job. Also, they are required to share this information with their colleagues.

**Continuous reinforcement.** A type of reinforcement which reinforces the desired behaviour each and every time it is demonstrated it occurs.

**Continuous service.** An uninterrupted period of service of an employee which may be interrupted on account of sickness, accident, leave, strike, lockout, lay-off or cessation of work not due to any fault of the employee.

**Contract.** A legal binding promise between two or more parties.

**Contract labour (regulation and abolition) act, 1970**. An act that attempts to regulate the employment of contract labour in certain establishments and abolishing it in certain other establishments. The main objectives of this act is that the system of contract labour should be abolished, wherever possible and practicable and in case the system could not be abolished altogether then the working conditions of the contract labour should be regulated so as to ensure payment of wages, and provision of the essential amenities.

**Contracting out.** Giving up the benefit of a statute. Usually, it is in the consideration of some alternative advantage or scheme.

**Contractual right.** A right based on a particular contractual agreement between the employer and the employee.

**Contrast error.** A performance appraisal error in which people are rated relative to others rather than against performance standards. For example, in a group of average performers, a person performing slightly above average is rated as best performer.

**Contributory plan.** A pension plan in which the money for the pension benefits is paid by both the employer and the employee.

**Controlled experiment.** A method to test the effectiveness of a training program that uses both a training group and a control group which receives no training. Data is collected both before and after the group is exposed to training and before and after a corresponding work period for the control group.

**Controlled industry.** Any industry the control of which by the union has been declared by any central act to be expedient in the public interest.

**Controlling.** A process of measuring actual performance comparing it with standards, finding deviations, if any and taking corrective actions. A process of ensuring that everything is moving in the desired direction.

**Controlling authority.** An authority appointed by either state or central government.

**Convenience sampling.** A type of non-probability sampling in which sample is obtained by selecting convenient population units. For example, sample obtained from readily available lists like telephone directories, etc. Also known as **chunk**.

**Conversion training.** The retraining of individuals for the occupation which is slightly different than the previous occupation, i.e., not radically or totally different.

**Cooling-off period.** A period of time during which the management is forbidden to declare a lockout or a trade union is forbidden to call a strike.

**Co-operation.** The willingness of the people to help each other.

**Co-operative society.** A society registered or deemed to be registered under the Co-operative Societies Act, 1912.

**Coordination.** To harmonise all the activities of an organisation in order to facilitate its working and its success. A rational and conscious process of pulling together the different parts of an organisation and unifying them into a team to attain the predetermined goals in an effective manner.

**Coordination training.** A 'team training' strategy that trains team members how to share the information and decisions in order to maximize team performance. This type of training is very significant for surgical teams and commercial aviation sector.

**Co-ownership.** The control of an organisation by its employees i.e., shared ownership.

**Co-partnership.** An arrangement in which all the persons working in an organisation share up to some extent in the capital, profits and control of the organisation.

**Copayment.** A payment made by the employee towards a portion of the cost of both medical care and the insurance premiums.

**Core competency.** An organisation's unique strength/capability that creates high value for the organisation and differentiates it from its competitors. For example, a firm's core competency may be highly skilled and committed workforce or strong financial base or technology superiority, etc.

**Core job characteristics.** The five job characteristics i.e., skill variety, task significance, task identify, autonomy and feedback, as identified by core job characteristics theory. They induce the critical psychological states needed for motivation at workplace.

**Core time.** A part of flexible work hours arrangement in which all the employees are expected or supposed to be at work.

**Core workers.** A firm's full-time employees. They enjoy privileges which are not available to contingent workers.

**Corporate campaigns.** A weapon in the hands of union in which union exerts pressure (financial, political or public) on the employees by pursuing firm's shareholders, directors, creditors, government agencies, firm's other unions.

**Corporate strategy.** The overall strategy which a company pursues. For example, strategy of rapid growth, to maintain and protect market, harness earnings and reinvest them elsewhere (strategy of an ageing company).

**Corporation**. Any body corporate established by or under any central, state or provisional act but it does not include a company or a co-operative society.

**Correlation analysis.** A statistical analysis which attempts to determine the association (degree of relationship) between two or more variables. The analysis involved three main steps: (i) determine whether a relation exists and if yes, then measure it; (ii) test whether it is significant; and (iii) establish the cause and effect relation, if any.

**Correlation coefficient.** A measure used to describe how well one variable is explained by another. It measures the degree of relationship between the two variables. It is represented by 'r' and its value can lies between $\pm$ 1. When $r = +1$, it means that there is a perfect positive correlation between the variables. And when $r = -1$, it means that there is perfect negative correlation between the variables. Also, in case $r = 0$, then it means there is no relationship between the two variables.

**Cost-benefit analysis of training.** An analysis of the costs and benefits associated with a training program. A comparison of costs and benefits is done in order to determine whether training is cost effective.

**Cost-of-living adjustment (COLA).** An American term that refers to pay raises which are tied to inflation indicators like consumer price index.

**Covered time.** The time spent on work for which piece-rate system or bonus exists but it is not used. Rather than payment by result, the payment is made on time basis.

**Coworker.** An individual with which an employee works who is neither his superior nor his subordinate.

**Craft union.** A union whose members are engaged in a single occupation or craft, usually using specialized skills.

**Creative conflict.** A concept that if the opposing views can be integrated rather than compromise then the conflict can be used as a mean of gaining the progress.

**Creative group.** A group of individuals in the organisation who provide creative ideas.

**Creativity.** The ability of an individual to produce new, novel and useful ideas.

**Creches.** A place where children are looked after, while their parents are at work. As per Factories Act, 1948*, in every factory* wherein more than 30 women workers are employed, there shall be provided and well maintained a suitable room(s) for the use of children under the age of 6 years of such women.

**Criterion-related validity.** Validity that demonstrates a substantial correlation between the test scores and performance scores. It shows that those who do well on the test also perform well on the job and *vice versa*.

**Critical incident method.** A method that focuses on keeping a record of certain critical behaviours (good or bad) behaviours of an employee which differentiates between an effective and non-effective job performance. These incidents are usually recorded by the superior as and when they occur and later on reviewed with the employee at predetermined timings.

**Cross-cultural preparation/training.** A process of educating the employees who are given foreign assignment. Preparations include knowing host country's history, culture, politics, economy, religion, business and social practices.

**Cross-functional team.** A group of employees, usually from the same hierarchical level, but from different functional/work areas, who come together to achieve a task.

**Cross-functional training.** A team training strategy in which employees are trained to perform operations in areas other than their assigned work. The team members are made to understand and practice each other's job.

**CTD.** Abbreviation for Cumulative Trauma Disorder*.

**Cultural change.** A change in the organisation's shared beliefs, aims and values.

**Cultural determinism.** It refers to the idea that one can infer/conclude an individual's values, interests, behavioural traits and motivations based on that individual's group memberships.

**Cultural immersion.** A behaviour-based program in which employees are send into the communities where they have to interact with the individuals from different cultures, races and nationalities.

**Cultural intelligence.** A person's awareness about the cross-cultural differences and his ability to function or adjust successfully in the cross-cultural situations.

**Cultural relativity concept of management.** A management concept that calls for molding management practices according to the workforce's different sets of beliefs, values, behaviours and attitudes of diverse workforce.

**Culture.** It refers to the totality of beliefs, knowledge, art, morals, customs, traditions and values. It is a cultivated behaviour, in a sense, that it is learnt from the other members of the society. Culture tells what is desirable and undesirable.

**Culture shock.** The inability of an individual to adjust to a different cultural environment. Difficulties include inability to understand local language, home sickness, lack of certain food supplies, products, etc.

**Cumulative trauma disorder (CTD).** An occupational injury that occurs when employees repetitively use the same muscles to perform the job (repetitively same physical movements). For example, data entry job, assembly-line job, etc.

**Currency.** The money in circulation in a specific country.

**Curriculum vitae.** A summary or an account of an individual's career provided by him while applying for a job. This includes his date of birth, educational qualifications, work experience, etc.

**Cyclical unemployment.** An unemployment which is caused by a downturn in the business cycle.

# D

**DA.** Abbreviation for Dearness Allowance.*

**Damages.** The compensation, in the form of money, awarded for the injury or loss suffered by a party.

**Danger money.** The more salary than usual salaries for doing dangerous jobs i.e., the jobs with whom illness or risk of accident is associated. So, additional salary associated with these jobs is danger money.

**Dangerous occupations.** Those occupations which involve hazards to the health or life of employees.

**Day.** A period of 24 hours beginning at midnight.

**Daywork.** The work which is performed mostly during day hours.

**DB.** Abbreviation for Defined Benefit*.

**DC.** Abbreviation for Defined Contribution*.

**DCI.** Abbreviation for Direct Computer Interviewing*.

**Dearness allowance (DA).** A special allowance (a system of payment) which is given in order to neutralize the high cost of living. It is used to protect the employee's real wage by neutralizing the increased cost of living. Usually, it is linked with cost of living index.

**Decentralisation.** It means dispersal of responsibility and decision-making authority throughout the organisation. It implies systematic efforts to delegate the authority from a central office to the lowest level or location that demands attention.

**Decertification.** A legal process in which a union is removed as the representative of a group of employees. Means termination of a union's right to represent the employees.

**Decision.** A course of action which is consciously chosen from among a set of alternatives to obtain a desired result.

**Decision-maker.** An individual who is formally responsible for making decisions in an enterprise.

**Decision-making.** A process of choosing a course of action from among a set of alternatives to achieve a desired result.

**Decision model.** A model the purpose of which is to provide a solution to a business problem. The model takes into account all the variables in a business decision, their relationships to each other, along with their constraints. For example, decision tree, linear programming model, etc.

**Decision support system (DSS).** A problem-solving system that helps the managers in the organisations to solve their problems. Usually, this system include "what-if" clause which allows its users to see how the outcomes or output changes when the data changes. For example, on the basis of different turnover rates, helping the organisations to determine the number and kind of new hires.

**Decision table.** A table used to help in making decisions. The table displays various problems which require action and the estimated probabilities of the outcomes of decisions.

**Decision tree.** A mathematical tool which enables a decisionmaker to consider various alternative courses of action and choose the best one. It is a graphic representation of various courses of action and associated risks with each action, and as it resemble a tree so-called as decision tree.

**Deductible.** An expenditure which an insurance policyholder must make or incur before the insurance policy makes any reimbursements. The employee would be responsible for the expenses from his own pocket before the insurance company makes any payment.

**Deferred annuity.** An annuity* in which the payments do not start at once but either after the policyholder attain a particular age or at a specified date.

**Deferred pension.** A pension that do no start at the normal time after retirement but sometime later and usually carry a higher rate of interest.

**Deferred profit-sharing plan.** A plan in which the employer credits a certain amount of profits to each employee's account (or to pension fund) which is payable at the time of employee's retirement, death or the termination of the service. In this plan, employer's contribution is regardless of the level of employee contribution.

**Defined benefit (DB) pension plan.** A retirement plan in which an employee is promised a pension amount based on a formula that considers employee's age and service.

**Defined contribution (DC) plan.** A retirement plan in which the employer promises to contribute a specific annual payment to employees' retirement or saving funds or account.

**Deflationary unemployment.** An unemployment that results from a general insufficiency of jobs. Also known as **involuntary unemployment**.

**Dejobbing.** The widening of the responsibilities of the organisation's jobs and encouraging the employees not to limit themselves to their job descriptions. Dejobbing results from the several changes taking place in the business world like globalized competition, political instability, technological developments, demographic changes, etc. Due to these changes, jobs are more and more difficult to define.

**Delayering.** The reduction in or removal of layers of job levels (usually middle management) from an organisation structure in order to achieve greater flexibility in the work assignments and in assigning merit increases.

**Delegation.** The act of passing authority and responsibility usually by a superior onto his subordinates.

**Deliberate sampling.** *See judgment sampling.*

**Delivery.** Under Maternity Benefit Act, 1961*, it means the birth of a child.

**Delphi technique.** A method of forecasting human resource (HR) needs in an organisation by collecting estimates of personnel needs from a group of experts (usually managers). In this method, human resource planning experts act as intermediaries, they summarize the various responses and then report the findings back to the experts for their opinions.

**Demand forecasting.** In context with HRM*, it refers to the process of estimating organisation's future quantity and quality of people required. Overall business plans and annual budget acts as a base for demand forecasting.

**Demarcation dispute**. The dispute between the trade unions (or sometimes between members of the same union) regarding the allocation of work between different types of workers.

**Democratic management.** A leadership or management style which is based on consultation and participation in the decision-making.

**Demography.** It is concerned with composition of population. For example, age, sex, martial status, etc.

**Demotion.** It means shifting an employee to a lower level where responsibilities and wages are less. It is just the opposite of promotion*.

**Demotion payment.** The payment given to the demoted employee in order to compensate him.

**Department.** It is a division or branch of an organisation.

**Departmentalization/departmentation.** A process of grouping of activities or work units into identifiable segments or departments. This grouping is based on the similarity of workflow or functional similarity.

**Dependant.** An individual who depends upon other person for his survival. For example, old people (especially without any pension) depend on their young employed children, a child depends upon his parents.

**Dependant benefit.** In case an insured person dies as a result of an employment injury sustained as an employee then his dependant will receive compensation under Employees State Insurance Act, 1948*.

**Dependent variable.** The variable which is affected by some independent variable.

**Depth interview.** An unstructured interview that involves the informal conversation between interviewer and the interviewee.

**Descriptive research.** A research which includes surveys and fact-finding enquiries of various kinds. The main purpose of this type of research is the description of state of affairs as it exists at present. Oftenly the term **Ex post facto** research has been used for descriptive research in business and social science research. The researcher has no control over the variables, he just report what has happened or what is happening.

**Deskilling**. A process of replacing individual skills by computers, information technology and other techniques in a operating system.

**Deterrance-based trust.** One of the types of trust in the organisational relationship in which the trust is based on fear of reprisal (act of retaliation) in case the trust is violated.

**Development.** An effort to improve employees' abilities which the organisation would need in the future. It is concerned with providing proper training through various methods.

**Development-oriented leader.** A leader who seek new ideas, value experimentation, generate and implement change.

**Deviant workplace behaviour.** Intentional antisocial acts of organisational members which violate the set norms and result in negative consequences for the organisation, its members, or both.

**Diagnostic skills.** The ability to find out the nature and circumstances of a particular condition. It is a capability to cut through the insignificant tasks and get to the heart of the problem i.e., logical thinking, analytical reasoning and creativity.

**Diagonal communication.** Communication between the people who are neither in the same department nor on the same level in the organisational hierarchy. This cuts across the departmental lines. In other words, it means communication between a manager and members of other work-groups. For example, a cost accountant incharge may ask directly the sales representative for the report.

**Diary (logs).** A method of collecting job analysis information in which the workers are made to record daily each activity in which they engaged along with the time of each activity. This detailed chronological nature of the log often supplemented with subsequent interviews of the workers and their supervisors.

**Dichotomous questions.** A question on a questionnaire which requires the respondent to tick one out of two answers, which are usually 'yes' or 'no'.

**Differential piece-rate system.** An incentive system in which employees earnings vary from minimum to maximum at different levels of output. For one part of the range, the earnings may vary proportionately less than the output and for the another part proportionately more.

**Dimension.** An aspect of performance which determines the effective work performance.

**Direct applicants.** The candidates who apply for a job vacancy in an organisation without any prompting from the organisation.

**Direct computer interviewing (DCI).** A method of interviewing that uses computer to conduct the interview i.e., the respondents interacts directly with the computer, which is programmed to ask questions and accept their responses.

**Direct financial payments.** A component of employee compensation that refers to pay in the form of salaries, incentives, bonuses and commission.

**Direct labour/worker.** The employees who are directly engaged in producing goods or services rather than those employees who carry out the other supporting activities (like staff functions).

**Direct labour cost (direct wages).** The expenditure on wages paid to those workers who are directly involved in the production of goods and services.

**Directing.** One of the managerial function which guides, motivates, supervises and lead people towards the attainment of planned targets of performance. It is concerned with execution of plans.

**Directive principles of state policy.** These are the guiding principles which the state ought to follow both while framing laws and enforcing them. They confer no legal rights and create no legal remedies, still they provide a good guidance to the state in the governance of the nation.

**Director.** A member of a board of directors who direct and control an organisation's affairs.

**Disabled person.** A person who has a physical or mental impairment that substantially restricts life activities.

**Disablement.** The loss of capacity to work or to move. This may result in loss or reduction of his earning capacity.

**Disablement benefit.** A benefit (under ESI Act, 1948*) that shall be payable to an insured person suffering from disablement as a result of an employment injury.

**Discharge.** To make a person free from a legal binding.

**Disciplinary action.** An action taken by employer against an employee for the violation of policy, rule, or regulations.

**Discipline.** A procedure which either corrects or punishes an employee when his any act or omission of any act violates a rule or procedure.

**Discovery method.** A method of teaching or training in which the work is so arranged that the trainee learns by himself rather than learning from the instructor.

**Discrimination.** To make a distinction. Laws prohibit making discriminations among the people on the basis of religion, sex, caste, colour or nationality.

**Disguised observation.** A research technique of matching and monitoring the objects, occurrences or people when the people do not actually know that they are being watched and their behaviour or action are noted.

**Dismissal.** A drastic disciplinary action which involves involuntary termination of a worker's employment with the organisation.

**Disparate impact.** A type of discrimination that occurs when a facially neutral employment practice disproportionately exclude a protected group from the employment opportunities. Facially neutral employment practice means a practice which otherwise lack the discriminatory content still it affects one group greater than the others. For example, for some reason employer hired persons on the basis of height (like air hostess, in army, etc.), employer's intention is not to discriminate anyone, yet by using height as a hiring factor naturally have a disproportionate impact on certain protected groups as women who are usually shorter than men.

**Disparate rejection rates.** A comparison of rejection rates for a protected group and the another group. This demonstrates that there is a discrepancy between the rates of rejection of a member of a protected (minority) group and the others.

**Disparate treatment.** A type of discrimination in which an employer treats a worker differently because of his protected-class status.

**Disposable income.** The income available with an individual for spending after making the payments of taxes, insurances and other required deductions.

**Disproportional stratified sampling.** A type of stratified random sampling* in which an equal number of cases is taken from each stratum regardless of how the stratum is represented in the universe.

**Dispute.** *See industrial dispute.*

**Dispute benefit.** The payment made by trade unions to the striking workers in order to compensate them for the loss of their wages.

**Dissonance.** An inconsistency (like in thoughts).

**Distinctive competencies.** The features or characteristics of a firm (like management system, value system, technical ability, image/reputation, goodwill, etc.) that gives it a competitive edge.

**Distributive bargaining.** A type of bargaining in which one party gains and the other loses. It is a zero-sum game as one party's gain is another's loss. This implies the strategy to grab as bigger share of the cake as it is possible.

**Distributive justice.** The perceived fairness in the distribution of outcomes. A facet of equity that examines how salary relates to performance. For example, two employees having almost similar performance records but one of them got a significantly higher salary rise than the other employee may perceive an inequity due to biasness, favouritism or some other factors not related with the job.

**Diversity.** Human characteristics (like friendly, intelligent, outgoing, introvert, extrovert, etc.) which differentiates people from one another.

**Diversity audit.** An assessment of a firm's effectiveness of diversity management program.

**Diversity training program.** A training program that provide diversity awareness and educate the employees on particular cultural and sex differences and also, how to respond well to these differences at the workplace.

**Division of work.** The work of every individual in an organisation should be limited, as far as possible, to the performance of a single leading function.

**Divisionalization.** The process of splitting a big organisation into separate divisions on the basis of geographical areas, products or services.

**Double employment.** The holding of two jobs by one individual.

**Downsizing.** A process of reducing, often dramatically, an organisation's workforce in order to improve its bottom line.

**Downward communication.** The flow of information in the organisation from a superior (higher level) to a subordinate (lower level). Oftenly used to issue instructions and orders to the employees. Also, used to dispose information regarding company's objectives, policies and programs.

**Downward move.** A change in job in which an employee is given less responsibility and authority.

**Draft.** A preliminary version of a document, later on after making the required changes it is finalized.

**Draw.** A system in which the salesman can draw advance payments against the future commissions. Later on, this amount drawn would be deducted from the future commission.

**DSS.** Abbreviation for Decision Support System*.

**Dual-career couple.** A couple whose both members have career issues at stake and both have occupational responsibilities. In the present era, the two-income family is fast replacing the single income family.

**Due process.** A just, fair and equal application of law, scheme or policy.

**Due process policies.** An organisation's policies that shows the formal steps which an employee can take to appeal against termination decision.

**Dues.** The subscription paid regularly in order to remain a member of some organisation. For example, a union.

**Duty.** A bigger work segment consists of various tasks that are performed by a person.

# E

**EAP.** Abbreviation for Employee Assistance Program*.

**Early retirement window offer.** An offer or opportunity that encourage employees to retire earlier. The term 'window' implies that the opportunity is open for the limited time.

**Earning-related pension.** See pension.

**E-business.** Abbreviation for Electronic Business*.

**Ecocentric management.** A management style which consider the environment related aspects as a core business concern. It considers the impact of business related activities on the natural environment as its responsibility.

**E-commerce.** Abbreviation for Electronic Commerce*.

**Economic strike.** A strike that takes place when both the parties (i.e., union and management) failed to reach on an agreement on the terms of the contract which includes wages, benefits, etc.

**Economic value added (EVA).** An organisation's net operating profit after the cost of capital is deducted. This approach requires that all organisational policies, measures and procedures should use the cost of capital as a benchmark against which the return is measured. Decisions related with human resources may be subjected to this analysis.

**EEO.** Abbreviation for Equal Employment Opportunity*.

**Effectiveness.** The achievement of goals and objectives.

**Efficiency.** The achievements of the goals with the least amount of resources.

**Efficiency ratio.** A ratio which measures the efficiency of an activity or labour over a period of time. The ratio is calculated by dividing the hours allowed by the actual hours taken for the production.

**Efficiency theory.** A theory of labour welfare according to which the welfare work is used as a mean to secure, preserve and develop the efficiency and productivity of workers. The theory emphasizes that the employer should take good care of his workers so that they become more efficient and productive. Also known as **functional theory**.

**Egalitarian pay system.** A compensation plan in which most of the employees of the organisation are the part of the same compensation system.

**E-HRM.** Abbreviation for Electronic Human Resource Management*.

**E-learning.** Abbreviation for Electronic Learning*.

**Electronic business (e-business).** A business which an organisation conducts electronically.

**Electronic commerce (e-commerce).** The buying and selling of products and services on the internet (online).

**Electronic human resource management (e-HRM).** The processing and transmission of information used in human resource management* (HRM) electronically. For example, posting of job openings online, online training, online selection test, online review of salary and bonus information, etc.

**Electronic learning (e-learning).** A training technique that takes the help of internet or organisation's intranet to conduct training online.

**Electronic mail (e-mail).** A type of electronic communication in which employees communicate with each other through written electronic messages sent through personal computer terminals linked by a network.

**Electronic mail survey (EMS).** A survey technique in which the respondents are sent questionnaire by group mail. They complete it and sent back to the researchers. This is fast, easy and cheap method of survey.

**Electronic meeting.** A group meeting in which the members interact on the computers. The members are presented with the issues, they type their responses on their computer screen, then the individual comments as well as the aggregate votes are displayed on a projection screen.

**Electronic performance support system (EPSS).** A computer-based training tool which automate training, documentation and phone support. Then it integrate this automatic into the actual application and provide a cheaper, faster and more effective support than the traditional methods.

**Electronic recruiting (e-recruiting).** The use of internet by the organisations for recruitment purpose.

**Elitist pay system.** A compensation plan that establishes different compensation plans by organisational level or employee group.

**E-mail.** Abbreviation for Electronic Mail*.

**Emoluments.** The amounts (monetary profit) received from an employment which includes all salaries, perks and other benefits.

**Emotional intelligence.** A person's ability to identify, understand and manage his emotions.

**Emotional labour.** A situation when workers express organisationally desired emotions during interpersonal transactions. For example, an air hostess is expected to be cheerful, a doctor to be emotionally neutral, etc.

**Emotional stability.** A personality dimension which characterizes an individual as self-confident, secure and calm.

**Employed person.** A person who works for an employer rather than being a self-employed person or an unemployed person seeking employment or being a non-employed person (i.e., who is neither in employment nor seeks for it).

**Employee.** Any person who is employed for wages.

**Employee advocacy.** A human resource manager's responsibility of defining how management should treat its employees, making sure that the employees can contest the unfair practices and also represents the employees' interests within the framework of its major obligation to the senior management.

**Employee assistance program (EAP).** A formal organisation-sponsored program that assists the employees to cope with personal problems which interferes with their work performance. The problems include alcoholism, drug abuse, stress, gambling and domestic violence.

**Employee attitude survey.** A formal survey designed to assess workers' likes and dislikes of various aspects of their jobs. Aspects include feelings about the work, supervisor, working conditions, advancement opportunities, training and development programs.

**Employee benefits and services.** The benefits that an employee receives in addition to the direct compensation. For example, health and life insurance. Often called as **indirect compensation** because they are provided to employees in the form of a plan (like life insurance) rather than cash.

**Employee buy-out.** A situation when the employees of an organisation acquire it or its branch. All the employees participate in its acquisition.

**Employee commitment.** An employee's identification with the organisation's mission and goals. An individual act as an owner rather as an employee.

**Employee compensation.** A package of rewards that an employee receives from his employment.

**Employee contribution.** An employee's contribution toward schemes like pension, saving plans, insurance, etc. in order to participate in the organisation benefit plans.

**Employee development program.** A program designed to upgrade employee's knowledge, skills and abilities (KSAs) in order to improve their performance and make them to advance successfully in their careers and within the organisation.

**Employee deviance.** The employees voluntary actions which violates the set norms and present threat to the organisation, its members, or both. For example, intentionally working slowly, leaving early, blaming co-workers, theft, gossiping, sexual harassment, sabotage and verbal abuse.

**Employee feedback program.** A program designed to improve employee communications by providing employees a voice in decision-making and also making sure that their complaints get redressed.

**Employee handbook.** A book provided by an employer to all of his employees which provides information on the employer-employee relations.

**Employee involvement program.** A formal participative program which utilizes the entire capacity of employee. It is designed in a way to encourage employees increased commitment to the organisation's success.

**Employee orientation.** A planned introduction of new employees to their jobs, their co-workers and the organisation.

**Employee-oriented leader.** One of the dimensions of leadership behaviour of the Michigan Studies that emphasizes the interpersonal relations. An employee-oriented leader will take a personal interest in the needs of the employees and accept the individual differences among the members.

**Employee ownership.** A situation when the persons working for an organisation own either some or sometimes all, of its shares.

**Employee participation.** 1. The appointment of employees' representative to board of directors in order to enable them to participate in business decisions. 2. For maintaining harmonious industrial relations by giving shares of the organisation in the workforce.

**Employee recognition program.** A program in which an organisation rewards its employees for their contributions and ideas. Formal employee recognition program include recognition, awards and suggestion systems.

**Employee relations.** The relations between an employer and his employees. The employees are considered as individuals, not as trade union members.

**Employee relations index.** An index of quality of relations between employee and employer. This involves assessment of factors like absenteeism, number of accidents, employee turnover, use of grievance settlement procedure, etc.

**Employee relations policy.** A policy designed to provide channel in order to resolve specific employee relations problems in the organisation before they become more serious.

**Employee relations representative.** A member of human resource (HR) department who acts as an internal consultant and ensures that organisation's policies and procedures are followed and guides both supervisors and employees on particular employee relations problems.

**Employee retirement income security act, 1974 (ERISA).** A U.S. Act that protects employees retirement benefits from the mismanagement. This is a major law in U.S. which governs the administration of retirement benefits.

**Employee separation.** The termination of an employee's membership from the organisation.

**Employee stock ownership plan (ESOP).** A plan that rewards the employees with the company stocks, either at a favourable price which may be below market price or as an outright grant.

**Employee welfare.** Anything done for the intellectual, moral, social, economic and physical betterment of the employees (whether by employer or by government or by other agencies) over and above the wages paid.

**Employees' provident funds and miscellaneous provisions act, 1952.** An act that provides for the institution of provident funds and family pension and deposit-linked insurance schemes for employees in factories and other establishments. The scheme of the act is to induce employees to save a portion from their present earnings for a rainy day.

**Employees' state insurance act, 1948 (ESI Act, 1948).** An act which is a piece of social security legislation in India. Its aim is to introduce social insurance by providing for certain benefits to employees in case of sickness, maternity, employment injury, etc.

**Employees' state insurance corporation (ESI Corporation).** A statutory body created to administer and execute the employees' state insurance scheme (ESI scheme). It is a body corporate having perpetual succession and a common seal.

**Employees' state insurance fund (ESI Fund).** A fund created (under ESI Act, 1948*) for the payment of benefits to the insured persons, meeting cost of administration and making provisions for other authorised purposes.

**Employer.** A person who provides employment to others.

**Employers' association.** An association of employers from different organisations, just like trade union of employees.

**Employer's liability.** The liability of employer to take all reasonable steps to protect health and safety of his employees and promote their welfare.

**Employer's liability insurance.** An insurance policy in which an employer has legal liability to pay the compensation to his employees in the event of any illness or injury during the course of their work.

**Employment agency.** An agency or an organisation which search the suitable candidates (employees) for the employers. For this task, it charges the employer a fee, generally related with the initial salary of concerned employee.

**Employment at will.** A rule long used by the employers to assert their right to terminate an employment relationship with an employee at anytime for any cause.

**Employment contract.** A contract that states clearly the terms and conditions of the employment relationship for both employee and employer.

**Employment costs.** The expenditure associated with employing people which includes their salaries, incentives, bonuses and other benefits.

**Employment injury.** A personal injury to an employee caused by an accident or an occupational disease arising out of and in the course of his employment.

**Employment interview.** An interview between the employer and the prospective employees in order to determine the suitability of the applicants for the job and organisation.

**Employment planning.** *See human resource planning.*

**Employment test.** Any employment procedure which is used as a basis for taking employment related decision.

**Empowering employees.** Putting employees incharge of what they do in the organisations. For this, managers need to learn how to give up their control and the employees have to learn how to take responsibilities.

**Empowerment.** Giving authority and responsibility to employees so that they can make decisions that were traditionally made by their supervisors or managers.

**EMS.** Abbreviation for Electronic Mail Survey*.

**Encapsulated development.** A mistake or a problem in the development program that occurs when a person learns new ideas and methods in a development course and then returns to a workplace that is still bound by the old methods and attitudes.

**Encounter phase.** A phase that occurs when an employee begins a new job. Although new employees are provided information about job and company during interviews but still in the beginning of their job, usually they experience surprise and shock.

**Enterprise.** An organisation in which some activity is carried out that involves risk and promises reward in return.

**Enterprise union.** A union that represents employees in only one big organisation rather than in a specific industry. For example, Japanese enterprise union. This ensures that union's loyalty will not be divided among the different organisations.

**Entrepreneur.** A senior manager or officer of a large organisation who takes the entrepreneurial approach to management, i.e., he takes risk and profit-oriented behaviour and usually, an incharge of a profit center created in the organisation.

**Environmental analysis.** An analysis of the organisation's external environment in order to identify the opportunities and threats in the environment. Also known as **environmental scanning**.

**Environmental challenges.** All the external forces that affect an organisation's performance but these are beyond the influence/control of the management. Also known as **environmental forces**.

**EPP.** Abbreviation for Executive Pension Plan*.

**EPSS.** Abbreviation for Employee Performance Support System*.

**Equal employment opportunity (EEO).** A government effort to ensure that all individuals, regardless of age, sex, race, disability, colour, religion, or national origin, have an equal opportunity for employment.

**Equal remuneration act, 1976.** The law that requires the payment of equal pay for equal work for both men and women in the same organisation.

**Equitable remuneration.** The fair and reasonable remuneration for employees in an organisation. Fair and reasonable payment is considered from the point of view of time and economic situation of the country.

**Equity.** A perceived fairness of the person's inputs with the output's received by the person.

**Equity theory.** A theory which states that employees perceive what they get from a job situation (outcome) in relation to what they put into it (inputs) and then compare their input-outcome ratio with the input-output ratios of relevant others (they may be one person like a colleague, a group like workers on the other shift, and/or someone from a previous or even hypothetical work situation). This theory was developed by J. Stacy Adams.

**E-recruiting.** Abbreviation for Electronic Recruiting*.

**ERG Theory.** A contemporary theory of motivation which states that there are three groups of core needs, existence (E), relatedness (R) and growth (G). This theory was developed by Clayton P. Alderfer. Existence needs includes both physiological and safety needs.

Relatedness needs align with Maslow's social need and the external component of Maslow's esteem classification. Growth includes the intrinsic component from Maslow's esteem category and the characteristics included under self-actualization.

**ERISA.** Abbreviation for Employee Retirement Income Security Act, 1974*.

**Ergonomics.** A study and design of the jobs to fit the physical abilities and characteristics of the employees. Adapting the working environment to employee safety and comfort needs.

**ESI act, 1948.** Abbreviation for Employees' State Insurance act, 1948*.

**ESI Corporation.** Abbreviation for Employees' State Insurance Corporation*.

**ESI Fund.** Abbreviation for Employees' State Insurance Fund.

**ESOP.** Abbreviation for Employee Stock Ownership Plan*.

**Esprit de corps.** The harmony and mutual understanding among the members of an organisation.

**Essential job functions.** All the job-related tasks and duties that every employee must do or must be able to do in order to become an effective employee.

**Establishment.** An organisation which employs a certain number of persons between whom and the organisation, the relationship of employee and employer comes to exist.

**Estimated work.** That work in the organisation for which standard times have been established without using work measurement techniques.

**Ethical behaviour.** The right, just, respected and good behaviour.

**Ethical dilemmas.** Those situations in which the employees are required to define right and wrong conduct.

**Ethnocentric approach.** An approach to manage the international operations of the firm in which top management and other key positions are filled by parent-country nationals (i.e., people from the home country).

**Ethnocentrism.** One's belief in the superiority of his own culture over the other cultures.

**EVA.** Abbreviation for Economic Value Added*.

**Executive.** An individual whose functions is to manage the affairs of the organisation.

**Executive director.** The director of the organisation.

**Executive order.** The orders passed or rules issued by the chief administrative authority in the organisation.

**Executive pension plan (EPP).** A pension plan for the executives or directors of an organisation in which the organisation gives a tax-deductible contribution in the premium.

**Executive share option scheme.** A share option scheme which allows executives or specified group of employees to buy company's shares.

**Exempt employee.** 1. An employee who is not liable under the Employees' State Insurance Act, 1948 to pay the employee's contribution. 2. An employee who is not covered by the provisions of the Fair Labor Standards Act (FLSA), 1938* of U.S. This includes executive administrative, professional and outside sales jobs. *See FLSA 1938.*

**Ex gratia.** The payment made out of kindness, gratitude, obligation, etc., and not for fulfilling any legal obligation.

**Ex gratia pension.** A pension* paid by an employer for which there was no legal, implied or contractual binding for providing it.

**Existence needs.** A core need group, under ERG theory*, which is concerned with providing the basic material existence requirements. This group of needs is similar to the lowest two needs of Maslow's need hierarchy*, i.e., physiological and safety needs.

**Exit interview.** An interview conducted to find out the reasons why the employee is leaving the organisation.

**Expatriate.** A citizen of one nation living and working in the other nation.

**Expatriation.** A process of preparing and sending employees to their foreign assignments.

**Expectancy chart.** A chart that shows the relationship between the test scores and job performance for a group of people.

**Expectancy theory.** A theory of motivation which states that the strength of a tendency to act in a certain way depends on the strength of an expectation that this act will be followed by a given outcome and on the attractiveness of that outcome to the individual.

**Expert system.** A computer system that imitate/mimic a human expert. It consists of three elements, a knowledge base (which contains facts and figures), a decision-making capability (drawing conclusion from facts and figures) and a user interface (which gathers and provide information to an individual using the system).

**Exploratory focus groups.** The focus groups which help in pilot testing, generating hypotheses and imprecisely defining the problem for further research.

**Exploratory research.** The preliminary research work in order to arrive at the exact nature of the concerned problem.

**Extended leave.** A benefit plan in which an employee can take a long-term leave from his office, while retaining all the benefits and the guarantee of a comparable job on his return in the organisation.

**External communication.** The communication of the organisation with the outside public.

**External environment.** The environment outside an organisation which affect it. For example, social, political, legal, natural environment, etc.

**External equity.** A perceived fairness in the pay relative to what other organisations are paying for the same period of work.

**External growth strategy.** An organisation's strategy that attempts to expand the organisation's resources or strengthening/raise its market share by mergers and acquisitions or by creating new businesses.

**External labour market.** All those persons who are outside the organisation and are actively looking for the employment.

**External recruitment.** The recruitment of candidates from outside the organisation. For example, campus recruitment, labour contractors, employment exchange agencies, etc.

**External sources of recruitment.** Those sources of recruitment which seeks suitable candidates from outside the organisation. These are advertisement, labour contractors, etc.

**Externals.** Those individuals who believe that their lives are controlled by outside forces like chances or luck.

**Externship.** An organisation following its employees to take a full-time operational role in the another organisation. This is a temporary assignment with the other organisations which acts as a good development strategy.

**Extra-mural welfare activities.** Those welfare activities or services which are undertaken outside the factories. For example, clubs, housing accommodation, educational facilities, etc.

**Extranet.** An internet-linked network which allows the employees to have access to the information provided by the external entities. For example, employees can submit their travel requests to an external travel service provider, can access their payroll information from the external payroll service provider, etc.

**Extroversion.** A personality dimension which describes a person who is sociable, and assertive in nature.

# F

**Facsimile transmission.** An economic method of sending written messages, copies of plans, documents, etc. on a fax machine. It is a widely used method of business communications, though e-mail is replacing this fax system. This system of sending written messages is popularly known as **fax**.

**Fact finder.** An independent person who studies the issues involved in a labour-management dispute, and makes a nonbinding recommendation for settling the dispute.

**Factor analysis.** A multivariate research technique which is used when there is a systematic interdependence among a set of observed variables. The researcher's main interest is in finding out something more fundamental that creates this interdependence or commonality among variables. The analysis put all the variables into few categories called as factors (based on the correlation between variables) and these derived factors are treated as new variables.

**Factor comparison method.** An analytical method of job evaluation that begins with the selection of factors (usually skills, effort, responsibility and working conditions), then ranking of jobs according to these factors, then adding together all these rankings to arrive at an overall numerical rating for each given job.

**Factories act, 1948.** An act that attempts to regulate the conditions of work in manufacturing establishments which come with in the definition of the term 'factory'. Specifically, it deals with the health, safety and welfare of workmen, working hours of adults and annual leave with wages and employment of women and young persons.

**Factory.** As per section 2(m), it means any premises including the precincts where (a) 10 or more workers are working or were working on any day of the preceding 12 months, and in any part of which a manufacturing process is being carried on with the aid of power, or (b) 20 or more workers are working or were working on any day of the preceding 12 months, and in any part of which a manufacturing process is being carried on without the aid of power.

**Fad.** A fashion which enters into market very quickly, people show great enthusiasm in adopting it and also declines fast. For example, fashion in dresses, new styles in clothing, etc.

**Fair day's work.** A concept given by Frederick Taylor that a fair day's work should depend on a formal, careful, scientific process of inspection and observation rather than vague supervisory estimates.

**Fair employment.** A situation in which employment related decisions of management are not affected by the illegal discrimination.

**Fair labor standards act, 1938 (FLSA).** A U.S. compensation law that requires employers to record earnings and hours worked by all the covered employees and to report this information to the U.S. department of labor. It defines two categories of employees, exempt and nonexempt.

**Fair wage.** A wage considered to be fair when it is equal to the prevailing rate in the same trade and in the neighbourhood for the similar work or if it is equal to the predominant rate for the similar work throughout the country. It is considered as something between a minimum wage and a living wage. While the lower limit of fair wage is usually the minimum wage the upper limit is set by mainly the capacity of the industry to pay.

**False negative error.** A selection error which means the rejection of an applicant who would have succeeded.

**False positive error.** A selection error in which an applicant is selected expecting success but later on failure occurs.

**Family.** According to ESI act, 1948*, it means all or any of the following relatives of an insured person, namely-a spouse, a minor legitimate or adopted child dependent upon the insured person, a child who is wholly dependent on the earnings of the insured person, a child who is infirm by reason of any physical or mental abnormality or injury and dependent parents.

**Family and medical leave act, 1993 (FMLA).** An American law that requires employers with 50 or more employees to provide up to 12 weeks' unpaid leave after childbirth or adoption, care for a sick spouse, child or parent or for an employee's own serious illness. FMLA* was enacted under the Clinton administration.

**Fatigue.** The feeling of tardiness and mental weakness. This decreases the workers level of performance at work.

**Fax.** *See facsimile transmission.*

**Federal violence against women act, 1994.** An American law through which a women seek relief for violent sexual harassment. The act requires that a person who commits a crime of violence motivated by gender shall be liable to the party injured.

**Feedback.** The information which is provided to the employees regarding their job performance. This is concerned with how well employees are meeting the objectives and goals.

**Feedback control.** A reactive approach of controlling the performance of a system by inspecting the output and then comparing it with the set standards. As this control is based on the past activities, nothing can be done about the not up to mark final output, only the care can be taken in future.

**Feedforward control.** A proactive approach of controlling the performance of a system which attempts to predict the future state of the system and takes the required action much before the actual problem arises.

**Fellow.** Associate members of a profession.

**Fidelity guarantee.** An insurance policy which covers the employers from any financial losses which they may sustain due to the employees dishonesty.

**Fiedler contingency model.** A contingency model of leadership which states that effective group performance depends on the proper match between a leader's style of interacting with subordinates and the degree to which the situation gives control and influence to the leader. This model was developed by Fred Fiedler.

**Field experiments.** The tests conducted for research purposes in the real environment, i.e., not in the laboratory.

**Field review method/theory.** An appraisal by someone outside the employee's own department, usually someone from the head office or the human resource department.

**Finders fees.** A form of monetary incentives which some organisation offers to its employees for suggesting a suitable or a successful referral. Also known as **referral incentives.**

**Fine.** A penalty in the form of money for wrongdoing.

**Firm.** A business organisation.

**First line supervisor.** A supervisor who is responsible for the management of employees at the shop floors.

**Fixed contribution pension.** A pension plan in which contribution to the plan is fixed and benefit depends upon the contributed amount.

**Fixed interval reinforcement schedule.** A reinforcement schedule which places rewards at the uniform time intervals.

**FJA.** Abbreviation for Functional Job Analysis*.

**Flash report.** A management report which focuses on key data that need corrective action.

**Flat benefit plan.** A plan whose benefits are unrelated to the earnings of the beneficiary.

**Flat organisational structure.** An organisational structure which has only a few levels of management.

**Flexibility.** The capability to adjust the system according to the changing environment.

**Flexible benefits program.** A benefit program in which employers allow their employees to select the benefits they prefer the most from a menu of choices. This is based on the concept that employees have diverse needs which requires different benefits packages. Also known as **cafeteria program.**

**Flexible staffing.** An arrangement that uses temporary workers, part-time workers, independent contractors and outsourcing. This type of arrangements are used in order to meet the workload fluctuations, working on a project with a definite end, replacing an absent employee, etc.

**Flexible time (Flex time).** A plan in which employees work for a set/decided number of hours per day but vary the starting and ending timings. For example, employees' workdays are build around core of midday hours, like 10 a.m.

to 1 p.m. They can determine their own starting and stopping hours, like they can work either 7 a.m. to 2 p.m or from 10 a.m. to 6 p.m.

**Flexible work hours.** A work arrangement that provides the employees control over their starting and ending times of their work schedule in the organisation. Flexible work hours divide the work schedule into 2 parts i.e., core time and flexible time (flex time).

**Floating labour.** A part of total regional or national workforce that has no stable employment but moves around both in terms of job category and geographic location.

**FLSA.** Abbreviation for Fair Labor Standards Act, 1938*.

**FMLA.** Abbreviation for Family and Medical Leave Act, 1993*.

**Focus group.** An exploratory research group consisting of 8 to 10 members who meet for a detailed or in-depth discussion on a specific topic. The group is led by a moderate who encourage them to have their full cooperation and maximum involvement. Usually all the discussions are recorded and observed later on to gain full knowledge of members.

**Focus group moderator.** An individual appointed by a research team who will lead a focus group.

**Force-field analysis.** A technique of identifying all the positive and negative forces acting on a problem.

**Forced choice method.** A performance appraisal method in which the rater is forced to select the readymade statements. In this, a series of statements about an employee is given to the rater and he has to indicate which statement is most or least descriptive of the employee.

**Forced distribution method.** A performance appraisal method which places a predetermined percentages of rates in various performance categories like excellent (10%), good (20%), average (40%), below average (20%), unsatisfactory (10%). This is based on the assumption that the employee performance level conforms to a normal statistical distribution (a bell-shaped curve).

**Forecasting**. The prediction about the future happenings. Identification of the expected future conditions with the help of past and present information.

**Foreign service premiums.** Financial payments, given to the employees on foreign assignments, above their regular base pay. Normally, it ranges between 10% & 30% of the base pay.

**Foreman.** The first line manager at the level of operation in an organisation.

**Formal authority theory.** According to this theory, authority originates at the top of an organisation and it flows downward through the process of delegation. So, the ultimate source of authority in an organisation lies with the shareholders.

**Formal education programs.** All the employee development programs. For example, short-term courses offered by professional institutes or universities, executive MBA programs, etc.

**Formal group.** A work group defined by the organisation structure. For example, an airline flight crew comprising of 8 members.

**Forming stage.** The first stage in group development process which is characterized by great uncertainty about the group's aim, purpose, structure and its leadership.

**Frame of reference.** A standard point or thing which serves as a comparison for the other points and so provides some meaning.

**Frame of reference training.** A form of training that uses fictitious examples of worker performance and presents these to the raters or supervisors and then ask raters to evaluate the workers in the examples and then inform them what their ratings should have been. Also known as **rater accuracy training**.

**Fraud.** A misrepresentation either by conduct or by a statement to achieve some advantage.

**Free interview.** *See depth interview*.

**Frequency distribution.** The classification of data into various class intervals.

**Frictional unemployment.** A type of unemployment which exists due to the time gaps (lags) between employees leaving one job and taking up the other job. For example, management students finishes their studies and enter the labour market, there might be chances of some delays in finding them all jobs in the labour market.

**Friendship group.** A group of individuals who share one or more common characteristics. For example, same age group, similar political views group, etc.

**Fringe benefits.** The benefits of rewards beyond the base pay of the employees.

**Full employment.** In context with human resources, a state when all the human resources of an economy are fully utilized or all are employed.

**Function.** A department of an organisation which carries out a separate activity. For example, human resource management, production, marketing, finance, etc.

**Functional authority.** The authority associated with a spęcific job.

**Functional control.** The authority exerted by a human resource (HR) manager as a coordinator of the personnel activities in the organisation.

**Functional job analysis (FJA).** A technique of the job analysis that attempts to describe the whole person on the job. FJA rates the job not just on the people, data and things but takes into account the extent to which specific instructions, reasoning judgment and mathematical and verbal ability are essential for performing the job tasks.

**Functional literacy.** An individual's skill level in a particular content area or field. For example, the ability to understand safety message, filling out order slips, etc.

**Functional strategy.** The contribution of individual functions towards the overall goals of an organisation.

**Functional theory.** *See efficiency theory*.

**Fund.** The sum of money held for a particular purpose. For example, provident fund, pension fund, etc.

**Fundamental attribution error.** A tendency to overestimate the influence of internal factors and underestimate the influence of external factors when making judgments about others behaviour.

**Funeral expenses.** The expenditure on the funeral of the insured person in case of his death. This is payable to the eldest surviving member of the family.

# G

**Gain sharing plan.** A plant wide (rather than organisation wide) incentive plan which engages the employees in a common effort in order to achieve productivity objectives and then share the gains. This is a form of group compensation based on the group or plant performance and which shares with the employees greater gains in productivity and/or profits.

**Game theory.** A type of decision theory based on choice of action, which is determined after considering all the possible alternatives available to the opponents playing the same game. It consist of players i.e., decisionmakers who have different goals. It studies those situations where two or more rational opponents are involved under conditions of competition and conflicting interests. For example, competitions in sports, elections, business, etc.

**Gantt chart.** A chart developed by Henry L. Gantt in 1917 which shows planned production in comparison with the actual production.

**Garnishment.** A court order that directs an employer to set aside a portion/part of an employee's wages to pay a debt owed to a creditor.

**Gatekeeper.** A manager in a big organisation who is concerned about the control of the flow of information in the organisation i.e., he takes decisions about passing the information downwards to a subsidiary or towards upwards (headquarters).

**Geared incentive scheme.** A scheme of payment by results in which the incentive payments go up in the stages instead of directly in proportion to output.

**General clerical test.** A psychological test developed in United States of America that measures numerical, verbal and clerical skills. This test takes about half an hour.

**General literacy.** An individual's general skill level (ability to read, write, speak, etc.).

**General manager.** A manager who is responsible for the overall administration in an organisation.

**General meeting.** A meeting in an organisation in which all the members of an association can participate.

**General strike.** A type of strike in which most of trade union in a nation participate and bring the whole nation to a standstill.

**General union.** A union that includes various industries and workers having different types of skills. They enjoy numerical superiority as they are open to all classes of workers and this is their strength. For example, national union of municipal and general workers.

**Generalizability.** A personnel selection method standard which refers the degree to which the validity of a selection method established in one context extends to the other contexts.

**Genetic monitoring.** The determination of the substances that are capable of causing damage to the genetic make up of the people. In this the harmful substances are brought out.

**Genetic testing.** A type of biological testing which is used to identify employees who are genetically susceptible to specific occupational substances/certain genetically based illness.

**Geocentric approach.** An approach to manage international business operations that seeks the best people for the key jobs throughout the organisation, regardless of their nationality. This staffing philosophy actively search best people on worldwide/global basis.

**Geometric mean (GM).** A statistical measure of central value and is defined as the nth root of the product of n items or values.

$$GM = \sqrt[n]{\chi_1 \times \chi_2 \times \ldots\ldots \times \chi_n}$$

**Gherao.** The encirclement of the employers or managers or supervisory staff with the intention to criminally intimidate them to accept the demands of the workers. Aim is to compel the persons to submit to the worker's demand without any recourse to the machinery provided by the law.

**Glass ceiling.** A barrier in an organisation that prevents women and minority employees from rising/advancing to higher-level jobs. This is a discriminatory practice.

**Global HRM.** *See international human resource management* (IHRM).*

**Global organisation.** An organisation that have its units or branches in a number of countries integrated to operate worldwide.

**Globalisation.** A tendency of the organisations to extend their manufacturing, ownership and/or sales to the foreign markets. Integration of national economy to the world economy and the world becomes a global market.

**GM**. Abbreviation for Geometric Mean*.

**Go slow strike.** A type of strike in which workers work very slowly than normal without actually stopping work. This is to bring the pressure on the management.

**Goal.** The desired state of affairs that an organisation wants to attain. It is the end what an organisation hopes to achieve.

**Goal obsession.** A term used in T-group or sensitivity training* for having too great concern for goals and too little concern with the existing behaviour patterns.

**Goal setting theory.** A theory of motivation which states that specific and difficult goals with feedback lead to higher performance. Motivation and performance are higher when an individual set specific, difficult but acceptable goals and when there is a feedback on performance.

**Going rate approach.** An approach to international compensation that links the base salary for international transfer/ expatriate to the salary structure in the host country. Usually, MNCs obtains information from the local compensation surveys.

**Golden handcuffs.** The financial incentives provided to key employees in an organisation in order to persuade them to remain in the organisation, in other words, so as to retain them.

**Golden handshake plan.** *See voluntary retirement scheme*.*

**Golden hello.** A payment made in order to persuade a prospective employee to join an organisation.

**Golden parachute.** A kind of benefit which provides protection and security to executives in case they lose their jobs or their companies are acquired by other companies.

**Good faith bargaining.** A type of bargaining in which both the parties (i.e., labour and management) makes every reasonable effort in order to arrive at an agreement. Both the parties communicate and match the proposals with counter proposals.

**Good faith effort strategy.** An employment strategy which is aimed at changing those practices that have contributed in the past in underutilizing the protected groups (i.e., women and minorities).

**Government grant.** The financial aid from the government side to an organisation in order to assist it in pursuing economically or socially desirable activities.

**Grade.** A classification system which contains jobs that are similar in difficulty but otherwise different. For example, mechanics, secretaries, firefighters, etc.

**Grade definition.** The written descriptions of the level, like effort, knowledge and responsibility required by the jobs in each grade. Then similar jobs can be combined into grades or classes.

**Grand strategy.** The overall strategy of a firm which aims at determining and communicating the probable shape which the firm is likely to take in future. Also known as **master strategy**.

**Grant-in-aid.** Any type of grant from the central government to a local authority for specific services in that area.

**Grapevine.** The informal communication in an organisation. It exists outside the formal communication channels in the organisation and is takes place through interpersonal contacts among the employees. It is unplanned, spontaneous, flexible, unstable, fast, unstructured, personal, social and directed towards the goals and need satisfaction of individuals.

**Graphic rating scale.** A scale on which a rater/evaluator has to mark an employee's performance on a continuum.

**Graphology.** A test designed to analyze the handwriting of a person. It attempts to predict the success or failure through one's handwriting.

**Gratuity.** A kind of retirement benefit (payment) which is given to an employee for his long and meritorious service. This payment intends to help an employee after his retirement. The amount payable in the form of gratuity to an employee shall not exceed Rs. 3,50,000.

**Gravy jobs.** The easy piece work jobs.

**Gray collar.** Those workers whose jobs lie in between blue-collar and white-collar jobs. They contain some elements of both.

**Green-circled employee.** That employee whose salary is below the range set for the job.

**Grievance.** Any complaint, formally stated in the writing, against the employer. This may be related with wages, working hours, working conditions, etc.

**Grievance arbitration.** When an impartial third party settle disputes regarding the different interpretations of a labour contract.

**Grievance procedure.** A systematic, formal step-by-step procedure which is designed to resolve the grievances. This refers to formal channels of communication to settle the disputes.

**Grievance settlement authority (GSA).** An authority set up for the settlement of industrial disputes connected with an individual workman employed in the establishment. An employer of every industrial establishment where 50 or more workers have been employed shall provide for a grievance settlement authority.

**Gross salary.** An individual's total salary before some deductions like income tax, group insurance contribution, provident fund, welfare fund and other applicable deductions.

**Group.** Two or more individuals who are interdependent and interact with each other and who have come together to achieve particular objectives.

**Group building methods.** Training methods that are designed to improve group or team effectiveness by helping the trainees to share their ideas and experiences, and understand the dynamics of interpersonal relationships and know their own strengths and weakness and those of their coworkers.

**Group demography.** The degree to which all the members of a group share a common demographic attribute like age, race, sex, educational level, length of service, etc. and the impact of this attribute on turnover.

**Group dynamics.** A social process in which people interact face to face in smaller groups. The forces operating within a group and their influence on the attitudes and behaviour of people are studied.

**Group incentive payment.** An incentive payment or scheme which is related with the work done by a group of workers, not individuals.

**Group interview.** An interview in which two or more candidates are interviewed simultaneously.

**Group life insurance plan.** An insurance plan, usually provided by most of the employers, that provides lower rates for the employer or employee and it includes all employees including the new employees.

**Group mentoring program.** A program in which an experienced senior employee is paired with a group of 4 to 6 junior (less experienced) employees. The senior person guides the junior employees in understanding the organisation and clarify their career directions.

**Group planning.** The planning for the specific groups or sections within a department or division. For example, advertising section, purchase section, etc. Also known as **sectional planning**.

**Group problem-solving.** A problem solving technique in which a supervisor or manager present a problem to a group of subordinates and ask them to find out a solution by mutual discussions.

**Group shift.** A change in decision risk between group's decision and the individual decision that each member within the group would make. In some cases, it can be conservative shift, in some cases a group may tend toward a risky shift.

**Group think.** A by-product of group decision-making in which the norm for consensus overrides the realistic appraisal of alternative courses of action. A situation in which the group pressures for conformity discourages the group from critically appraising unusual views. It is a sort of disease which hinder the group performance.

**Groupware.** A software that allows the multiple users to share, track and organise information and work on the same document simultaneously. This is used by organisations in order to improve business processes like account management, sales management, etc.

**Growth.** The expansion of an economy. The increase in national income is usually considered as a growth in the economy.

**Growth industry.** Any industry which is predicted to grow faster than the others in future.

**Growth needs.** A core need under ERG theory* which is concerned with the individual's intrinsic desire for personal development. These needs relate to the development of human potential. These needs include the intrinsic component of Maslow's esteem category and the characteristics included under self-actualization*.

**Growth strategy.** A firm's strategy of expansion and diversification. This is a risky strategy and should be well forecasted.

**GSA.** Abbreviation for Grievance Settlement Authority*.

**Guaranteed minimum pension.** An amount which is guaranteed to be paid after the retirement of a person under a pension scheme. The actual amount in the form of pension may be higher than this but never lower payment.

# H

**Haggle.** A process of arguing or discussions or bargaining about the price or other terms.

**Halo effect.** A situation when one aspect or trait of an individual's performance influences or biases the evaluation of the entire performance of the individual. When the influence is favourable, it is called halo effect, and when the influence is unfavourable then it is called as **horns effect**.

**Handicraft system.** A system or practice of engaging in a trade in a small shop mostly by hand or with the help of very simple machinery.

**Harassment.** The actions and/or words which are unlawful and anti-social.

**Hard core unemployed.** The people who are unemployed as they lack the essential educational qualifications or skills needed by the economy.

**Hard goals.** The goals that are objective, quantifiable and can be directly measured. For example, return-on-investment (ROI), market share, net profits, etc.

**Hardship allowances/premium.** A key component of an international compensation program. It compensates the expatriates for hard living and working conditions at foreign locations. In other words, it is a salary premium as an inducement to accept a foreign assignment or a compensation for any hardship caused by foreign assignment. Also known as **foreign service inducements**. These are paid in the form of a percentage of salary, usually 5-40 per cent of basic pay.

**Hawthorne experiments.** Conducted by Prof. Elton Mayo, these experiments show the overwhelming influence of psychological and social factors on employee morale and productivity. After these findings, the jobholder becomes the focus of attention rather than the job itself.

**Hazardous process.** Any process or activity where, unless special care is taken raw material used therein or the intermediate or the finished products, by-products, effluents, or waste would cause material impairment to the health of the persons engaged in/connected or result in the pollution of the general environment.

**HCN.** Abbreviation for Host Country National*.

**Head hunters.** The employment agencies who are expert in searching suitable executives for an organisation, or search suitable jobs for the executives who desire to change their existing job.

**Health.** A state of physical, mental and emotional well-being. A state of being free from illness. A sound condition of mind or the body.

**Health maintenance organisation (HMO).** A pre-paid health care plan that provides comprehensive medical services/benefits as well as preventive medicine for employees and their families, who pay a nominal fee in addition to the fixed annual fees paid by the employer.

**Health promotion.** An approach to encourage and facilitate the employees to enhance healthy lifestyle.

**Heuristics.** The judgmental shortcuts taken by individuals in decision-making in order to avoid information overload.

**Hidden unemployment.** *See concealed unemployment.*

**Hierarchy of needs theory.** A hierarchy of five needs—physiological, safety, social, esteem and self-actualization, as one need is satisfied substantially, then the next need becomes dominant.

**High context cultures.** The culture which rely heavily on the nonverbal and subtle situational cues during communication. Countries such as Japan, Korea, Vietnam, China are high-context cultures. In these cultures, what is not said becomes more significant than what is actually said. For example, a person's reputation, official status, etc.

**High-leverage training.** The training which is linked to the strategic business objectives and goals, uses an instructional design model, has top management support and compares the organisation's training programs against the training programs in other organisations.

**High performance work design/ system.** A work system that concentrates on setting up working groups in the environments where high levels of performance are required. This system maximizes the fit between employees and technology.

**High potential employees.** Those employees which the organisation believes are capable of being successful in the higher level managerial positions like CEO, general manager of business unit, etc.

**Higher order needs.** The needs which are satisfied internally (i.e., within the person). These are social, esteem and self-actualization needs.

**HIP.** Abbreviation for Human Information Processing*.

**Hiring freeze.** An employment policy which is designed to reduce an organisation's workforce by not hiring any fresh/new employees into the organisation.

**Histogram.** A graph or a bar chart which consists of a set of vertical bars whose areas are proportional to the frequencies they represent.

**HMO.** Abbreviation for Health Maintenance Organisation*.

**Horizontal communication.** The flow of information, opinions and ideas among the positions at the same level of authority. For example, a meeting between marketing manager and production manager. Communication among the peers help to improve coordination, mutual understanding and teamwork among different departments of the organisation. Also known as **lateral communication**.

**Horizontal integration.** A situation when all the business activities are carried out at the same stage in the production process. Also known as **lateral integration**.

**Horizontal mobility.** A form of labour mobility in which there is no change in the status. *See mobility of labour also.*

**Horns effect.** *See halo effect.*

**Host country.** A country in which the parent country company attempts to locate its business unit/branch or has already located its unit.

**Host country national (HCN).** An employee working for an organisation, is a citizen of the country where the operation of the organisation is located. The headquarters of the organisation are in the another country. For example, the Indian multinational Tata employs British citizens in its British operations.

**Hostile work environment (sexual harassment).** It occurs when the behaviour of anyone at the workplace is sexual in nature and is perceived by an employee as undesirable and offensive. These offensive conditions unreasonably affect an individual's work performance or psychological well-being.

**Hot-stove rule.** This is a model of disciplinary action. This suggests that discipline should be immediate, provides ample/sufficient warning and be consistently applied to all employees.

**House journal.** An organisation's own journal for its employees that usually contains information like company news, policies, etc. for informing its employees, making them aware of organisation's latest happenings.

**HR.** Abbreviation for Human Resources*.

**HRA.** Abbreviation for Human Resource Accounting*.

**HRD.** Abbreviation for Human Resource Development*.

**HRIS.** Abbreviation for Human Resource Information System*.

**HRM.** Abbreviation for Human Resource Management*.

**HRP.** Abbreviation for Human Resource Planning*.

**Human capital.** The education, knowledge, skills, training abilities and expertise of an organisation's employees.

**Human communication.** A process of communication between people.

**Human engineering.** *See ergonomics.*

**Human information processing (HIP).** An examination of the various processes involved in business decision-making.

**Human relations.** The social and psychological relations among people at workplace.

**Human resources (HR).** The people who work in an organisation. Also known as **personnel**.

**Human resource accounting (HRA).** A process of identifying and measuring data about human resources and reporting this information to the interested parties. Data includes costs incurred to recruit, hire, train, develop and maintain employees and their present economic value to the company. In other words, it is assessment of costs and values of the people as organisation's resources.

**Human resource audit.** Analysis of present employees' skills and abilities. Human resource planners have a detailed summary of the capabilities available in the organisation. The audit may include one department or an entire organisation, usually it involves the evaluation of the human resource department itself.

**Human resource development (HRD).** A part of human resource management function which is concerned with training and development, career planning and development, organisation development, performance appraisal, potential appraisal and development, rewards and employee welfare. HRD is the development aspect of HRM.

**Human resource generalist.** An individual who has the responsibility of performing a variety of human resource activities.

**Human resource information system (HRIS).** A systematic procedure used to collect, record, store, maintain, analyze, retrieve and distribute the information related to the organisation's human resources.

**Human resource management (HRM).** It is the planning, organising, directing and controlling of the procurement, development, compensation, integration, maintenance and separation of human resources up to the end so that the individual, organisational and social objectives are achieved.

**Human resource manager.** A generalist who administers and co-ordinates various programmes cutting across the functional areas. Usually, he is a top-ranking person at a plant, who is expected to have knowledge about all areas of HRM*.

**Human resource planning (HRP).** A process by which an organisation ensures that it has the right number and kind of people, at the right place, at the right time, capable of effectively and efficiently completing those tasks that will help the organisation to achieve its overall objectives. Also known as **employment planning or personnel planning.**

**Human resource research.** The analysis or the study of the data obtained from the human resource records in order to determine the effectiveness of the past and present human resource practices.

**Human resource specialist.** An individual who has in-depth / detailed knowledge and expertise in a limited area of human resources. For example, great knowledge of activity or area of training, selection tests, compensation, etc.

**Human resource strategies.** An organisation's use of its human resources in order to gain competitive advantage against its competitors in the market.

**Human resource tactic.** A particular human resource program that attempts to advance an organisation's strategic goals and objectives.

**Human skills.** The ability to work effectively with the other people both as individuals and as members of a group. These skills are required to win co-operation of others and to build effective work teams.

**Humanitarian.** Promotion or improvement of human welfare and reducing their sufferings.

**Hush money.** The money given to a person in order to persuade him to remain silent on some specific matter. For example, when an employee discovers some wrongdoing at workplace is paid by management to prevent him going to appropriate authority or going to inform public.

**Hygiene factors.** One of the two factors of Frederick Herzberg's two-factor theory. These include company policy and administration, supervision, salary, security, status, working conditions and interpersonal relations. When workers were dissatisfied they tend to attribute to these extrinsic factors. And when factors are adequate, they will not be dissatisfied. Also known as **maintenance factors/job-context factors/dissatisfiers**.

**Hyper employment.** A situation when the demand for labour greatly exceeds the supply. For example, situation during inflation. Also known as **overall employment**.

**Hypothesis.** An assumption which a researcher make about a population parameter. It is a supposition made as a base for reasoning.

**Hypothesis testing.** To test some hypothesis about the population from which the sample is drawn. The procedure involves, setting of a hypothesis, setting of a suitable significance level, setting the test criterion, making calculations and taking decisions.

# I

**Identification based trust.** One of the types of trust in organisational relationships in which trust is based on the mutual understanding of each other's intentions and the appreciation of the other's desires. This type of trust allows one party to act as an agent for the other and substitute for that individual in interpersonal transactions.

**Idle time.** The time during which an employee is paid but actually have not done any productive work for employer.

**IHRM.** Abbreviation for International Human Resource Management*.

**Illegal bargaining items.** Those items in collective bargaining which are forbidden by law.

**Illegal issues.** Those collective bargaining issues that would require either party (labour or management) to take illegal action. In case one party wants to bargain on these issues, the other one can refuse. For example, giving preference to the trade union members while hiring employees.

**ILO.** Abbreviation for International Labour Organization*.

**Image.** The mental perceptions held by a person about himself, about others or about the various products or services.

**Imaging.** Scanning the documents, then storing them electronically and retrieving them, whenever required later on. For example, scanning applicant's bio-datas and storing them in a database and accessing them, whenever need arises.

**Immediate annuity.** An annuity* contract which starts making payment as soon as it comes into force.

**Immediate confirmation.** A concept which emphasizes that people learn best when reinforcement and feedback is given just after training.

**Immediate employer.** A person who has undertaken the execution of the work of the principal employer. He may have undertaken the responsibility of the execution of the work independently or under the supervision of the principal employer or his agent.

**Immigrant remittances.** The money sent by the immigrants to the native nation (back home) to families from the nation where they live and work.

**Impasse.** A situation in collective bargaining when both the parties are unable to move forward toward settlement. An impasse usually occurs in case one party is demanding more than the other party can offer.

**Implied authority.** The authority exerted by a human resource manager by the virtue of others' knowledge that he has access to the top management in the organisation.

**Implied term.** In a contract, it is a provision which is presumed but not agreed in writing by the parties to the contract.

**Importing and exporting.** The purchasing and selling goods and services in the other countries.

**In-basket exercise.** A simulation exercise about the administrative tasks of a manager's job. This is one of the off-the-job employee training and development program. The participants study a variety of documents (for example, reports, letters, memos) that may appear in-basket of a manager's desk, and then decide how to respond to them.

**In-house development center.** An organisation-based method to develop improved management skill in the prospective managers by realistic exercises.

**Incentive.** The variable monetary reward paid to employees according to the variations in their achievement (or performance). Also known as **payment by results**.

**Incentive stock option.** A right given to the employees in organisation to purchase a specified number of shares of the organisation at a given price during a given period.

**Incentive system.** A system of payment that provide extra pay for extra performance in addition to regular wages for a job. Also known as **incentive plan or scheme**.

**Income.** Any amount which a person or an organisation receives as a reward for the effort or as a return on investment.

**Income in kind.** *See benefits in kind.*

**Income policy.** A policy of the government which attempts to control the inflation and keeping full employment by holding down the raises in wages and prices by some direct or indirect statutory measures.

**Increment.** An amount added automatically in the pay scale of a person.

**Incremental payment system.** A payment system in which increments are given which may arise from age or merit.

**Independent contractors.** Those employees who perform particular/ specific services on contractual basis.

**Independent variable.** A variable that brings some change in the dependent variable.

**Indian labour conference.** A tripartite body consisting of representatives of employers, employees and government set up for discussions and consultation on matters relating with labour.

**Indirect financial payments.** A component of employee compensation that includes pay in the form of financial benefits like insurance, vacations, etc.

**Indirect labour.** 1. Those employees of an organisation who directly does not produce goods or services which that organisation sells in the market. For example, cleaners, office staff, etc. 2. A contractor's employees who work for another organisation.

**Individual centered career planning.** A career planning that concentrates on individual's career rather than on organisational needs and requirements. This type of career planning is performed by the employees themselves by analyzing their own individual goals and skills.

**Individual challenges.** Those human resource issues that address the decisions most relevant to individual employees.

**Individual equity.** The fairness in pay decision of employees.

**Individual retirement account (IRA).** An account in which an employee can put funds and which will not be taxed until the employee retires from the job.

**Individual training methods.** The training methods for individuals as opposed to groups. For example, personal job instruction, programmed instructions on computer.

**Individualism-collectivism.** This is one of the Geert Hofstede's cultural dimensions that describes the strength of relation between an individual and other individuals in the society (i.e. the degree to which the people act as individuals rather than as members of a group).

**Individuals with disabilities.** The people who have a physical or mental impairment which virtually affects life's major activities.

**Induction.** The introduction of a new employee to the organisation. New employees are welcomed when they first join the organisation and are provided basic information about job and organisation. Also known as **orientation**.

**Industrial democracy.** Any system which allows workers to participate or express/share their views on various work-related matters in an organisation. For example, works committee, unit council, joint council, workers participation in board of directors, etc.

**Industrial dispute.** According to section 2(k) of Industrial Disputes act, 1947*, it means any dispute or difference between (i) employers and employers, or (ii) employers and workmen, or (iii) employers and workmen, which is connected with (a) employment or non-employment, or (b) the terms of employment, or (c) the conditions of labour of any person.

**Industrial dispute act, 1947.** An act that attempts to secure industrial peace by preventing and settling industrial disputes between the employers and employees with the help of machinery (like works committee, conciliation machinery, adjudication and arbitration).

**Industrial establishment.** An establishment or an undertaking where industry* is carried on.

**Industrial harmony.** The existence of understanding, co-operation and a sense of partnership between the employers and the employees. It is considered as a positive concept.

**Industrial law.** All the statutes and case law pertaining to industry*.

**Industrial medicine.** An employer's health care provision for his employees. For example, provision of best possible working environment, first aid services, regular health checkup, etc.

**Industrial peace.** It emphasizes the absence of struggle and strife. It is considered as somewhat negative and restrictive concept in comparison to industrial harmony.

**Industrial psychology.** The application of psychological concepts to the problem of persons working in the industry.

**Industrial relations.** The collective relationship between employer, employees and government in any organisation. The concept of industrial relations is a dynamic concept, which keeps on changing according to the development of new situations.

**Industrial tribunal.** A tribunal set up under Industrial Disputes act, 1947*, by the appropriate government*, for the adjudication of industrial dispute relating to any matter, whether specified in the second schedule or the third schedule. Matters (in third schedule) include wages, compensatory and other allowances, hours of work, rest intervals, leave with wages, holidays, bonus, profit-sharing, gratuity, provident fund, shift working, rationalization, discipline rules, retrenchment, closure of establishment, etc.

**Industrial union.** The union which include the persons working in the same industry regardless of the jobs held by them.

**Industry.** According to section 2(j) of Industrial Disputes Act, 1947*, it means any systematic activity carried on by co-operation between an employer and his workmen.

**Infant industry.** The newly set up industrial units.

**Informal communication.** *See grapevine.*

**Informal group.** A group which is neither formally structured nor organizationally determined but arises or formed in response to the desire for social contact. For example, workers from different departments having tea together during breaks.

**Informal training.** The training which occurs by the interactions and feedback among the employees in the organisation.

**Information dissemination.** A process of making information available to the decisionmaker at various levels in the organisation. Methods of disseminating information include written communications, meetings, employee handbooks, etc.

**Information overload.** A situation in which the information inflow exceeds a person's processing capacity.

**Information ownership.** The unique information and knowledge about the jobs possessed by the individuals in the firm. For example, supervisor may have a specific effective way of handling conflict among the employees. Usually, individuals do not like to share this information and knowledge with the others.

**Initiating structure.** It is one of the dimension of Ohio State Studies which refers to the extent to which a leader is likely to define and structure his role and those of his subordinates in the search for goal accomplishment. A leader high in initiating structure will expect employees to maintain definite standards of performance, emphasizes meeting the deadlines and assign group members to particular tasks.

**Injunction.** Under U.S. law, this means a court order that compels a party or parties either to resume or to desist from a certain action.

**Inside director.** An employee of an organisation who has been appointed to the board of directors.

**Inside games.** A union tactic to convince the employees to distrupt or to obstruct the production. For example, by refusing to over-time, by slowing down the pace of work, etc.

**Instrumental values.** Means of achieving a person's terminal values. These are preferable modes of behaviour. *See terminal values also.*

**Insubordination.** A form of misconduct which includes willful disobedience or disregard of the boss's authority. This also includes public criticism of boss, verbal abuse of the boss, deliberate defiance of stated firm's policies and rules, disregard for the chain of command and involvement in an effort to undermine and even remove the boss from the power.

**Insurable employment.** An employment in a factory or establishment to which employees state insurance act, 1948* applies.

**Insurance.** A legal contract in which one party known as insurer* promises to pay a particular amount to another party, known as insured*, in case a specified event happens (for example, accident, fire, loss-of-profit, etc.) and due to which the insured suffers a financial loss. As per the contract, the insured has to pay a specific amount of money, called as premium, either once or twice a year or at some other regular intervals.

**Insurance policy.** A document which contains the terms and conditions of an insurance contract. It states the premiums required and the benefits payable.

**Insured.** An individual or a company who are covered by an insurance policy. Those policies which covers the death, then the alternative word assured is usually used for that person in the event of death of the assured person.

**Insured person.** Under Employees State Insurance Act, 1948*, it means a person who is or was an employee in respect of whom contribution are or were payable as per this act and who is entitled to any of the benefits provided by this act.

**Insurer.** An individual or a company or other organisation which undermines an insurance risk.

**Integrated disability management program.** A benefit which combines the disability insurance programs and efforts in order to reduce the employee's insurance claims. It helps in cost savings and in better coordination.

**Integrated learning system.** A planned learning system which combines the use of a number of methods of instruction and teaching aids.

**Integration.** A function of human resource management which deals with the integration of individuals, societal and organisational goals. Mainly, it focuses on good labour-management relations, grievance handling and maintenance of discipline and free flow of communication at all levels.

**Integrative bargaining.** A type of bargaining that focuses on expanding the size of the cake with both the parties getting continuously a bigger share. This aims at convincing the other party that benefits of mutual agreement on proposed terms would be very high.

**Intellectual ability.** An individual's capacity to perform mental activities. For example with the help of intelligence quotient (IQ) tests, a person's general intellectual abilities are measured.

**Intellectual capital.** An intangible source of value in an organisation that refers to productivity, service and creativity provided by the employees.

**Interacting group.** A group in which the members interact with each other face to face. They rely on both verbal and nonverbal interaction to communicate with each other.

**Interactional justice.** A concept of justice that refers to the interpersonal nature of how the outcomes were implemented. The four key determinants of interactional justice are explanation (emphasize those aspects of procedural fairness which justify the decision), social sensitivity (treating the individual with full dignity and respect), consideration (listening to the individual's concerns) and empathy (identifying with the individual's feelings).

**Interest group.** A group comprising of individuals who may affiliate with one another in order to achieve a particular objective with which each member is concerned. For example, to support a suspended colleague, to form a united body to further their interests, etc.

**Interest inventory.** A selection tool which compares an individual's present interests with those of others, know-how in various occupations in order to determine the most preferred occupation for the individual.

**Interest rate.** The amount paid by a bank or other financial institution to a depositor of funds, expressed as percentage of the amount deposited. Also, the amount charged on a loan, expressed as a percentage of the sum borrowed.

**Intermittent reinforcement.** A type of reinforcement which reinforces the desired behaviour often to make the behaviour worth repeating but not each and everytime it occurs/is demonstrated.

**Internal analysis.** An analysis of an organisation's strength and weaknesses.

**Internal audit.** An audit conducted by an organisation on its own behalf to ensure that its own internal controls are working satisfactorily.

**Internal control system.** An organisation's own system of controls comprising both financial and non-financial which ensures that it carries out its business in an orderly, efficient and effective manner.

**Internal equity.** The perceived fairness of the pay structure within an organisation.

**Internal growth strategy.** An organisation's strategy that focus on new market, innovation, joint ventures, mergers and acquisitions and product development.

**Internal labour force.** Labour force of current or present employees in the company.

**Internal recruitment.** Looking for the applicants from those who are currently employed with the firm. For example, employee referrals, present employees, former employees, etc.

**Internals.** All those individuals who believe that they control their destinies.

**International human resource management (IHRM).** A process of procuring, allocating and effectively utilizing human resources in an international business.

**International labour organisation (ILO).** An international labour organisation, established under the Treaty of Versailles, was created in 1919. It works for the establishment of lasting peace on the basis of social justice*. Its main principles include (i) labour is not a commodity, (ii) freedom of expression and of association are necessary for sustained progress, and (iii) poverty anywhere constitutes danger to prosperity everywhere. India is a founder member of ILO.

**International uniformity.** A fundamental principle of labour law that postulates enactment of labour laws with a view to give effect to the provisions of resolutions, adopted by international organisations like ILO*, United Nations and other similar international bodies. The countries ratifying the resolutions or agreements are under the obligation to enforce them.

**Internet.** A world-wide network of computers connected to each other by telephone cables, satellite links, modems, etc.

**Interview.** A formal, in-depth conversation conducted in order to assess an applicant's acceptability. This allows a two-way exchange of information, on one side, the interviewers learn about the applicant (skills, work experience, career plans) and on the other side, the applicant learns about the employer and the organisation.

**Interviewer error.** An error on the part of the interviewer due to conscious or unconscious bias. For example, he may assume that if someone's hobby is the game of chess then he is highly intelligent, etc.

**Intramural welfare activities.** All those welfare activities which are undertaken inside the factories. For example, canteens, crèches, rest rooms, washing and bathing facilities.

**Intranet.** A company network which operates over the internet.

**Intraorganisational bargaining.** The bargaining on the conflicting objectives of factions within the labour and management, it is a part of the labour-management negotiation process.

**Intrinsic value.** A value that something has due to its basic nature.

**Intuition decision-making.** An unconscious process which is created out of distilled experience.

**Intuitive.** An individual's feelings which are not necessarily supported by the research.

**Involuntary separation.** A separation which occurs when an organisation decides to terminate its relationship with an employee. This may be due to economic reasons or due to poor fit between the employee and the organisation.

**Involuntary turnover.** The employee turnover initiated by the employer.

**ISO 9000.** The written quality standards adopted worldwide. These standards were developed by international organisation for standardization (ISO) based in Geneva, Switzerland. ISO 9000 represents a family name of standards (ISO 9000, 9001, 9004, etc.).

**ISO 9001.** A comprehensive quality standard that covers product or service design and development, manufacturing, installation and customer service.

**ISO 9004.** A quality standard which provides a guide for the organisation that wants to make improvement.

# J

**JCQ.** Abbreviation for Job Compatibility Questionnaire*.

**JDI.** Abbreviation for Job Description Index*.

**JIT.** 1. Abbreviation for Just-In-Time management*. 2. Abbreviation for Job Instruction Training*.

**Job.** The grouping of duties, tasks and responsibilities which constitute a total work assignment for the employees.

**Job aids.** The sources of information (such as set of instructions, pamphlets, diagrams, reference guides, etc.) that are available at the job site to guide the workers quickly while making a decision or performing a specific task. For example, a checklist of things to do before a take off for airline pilots.

**Job analysis.** The systematic process of studying and collecting information regarding the duties and skill requirements of a specific job. It identifies the duties, tasks and responsibilities of a specific job. Its immediate products are job descriptions and job specifications.

**Job banding.** An approach of replacing narrowly defined job descriptions with broader categories (or bands) of related jobs in the organisation. In this approach, the organisations usually collapsed the various job titles to just few with increase in range of pay along with increased responsibility.

**Job card.** A card that records the details about a particular job. For example, the machines and equipments used, number of total units produced, etc.

**Job characteristics model.** A model that shows how job design affects employee reactions. In this model, jobs can describe in terms of five characteristics, i.e., skill variety, task identity, task significance, autonomy and feedback.

**Job classification method.** An approach of categorizing the jobs into groups. Also known as **job grading.**

**Job compatibility questionnaire (JCQ).** A questionnaire that determine whether an applicant's preferences for the work matches with the characteristics of the job. JCQ collects information on all aspects of a job which have bearing on worker performance, turnover, absenteeism and job satisfaction.

**Job costing.** A practice which allocates the costs to the particular job.

**Job criteria.** All the key or important elements in a given job.

**Job cycle.** A complete sequence of various operations which an employee performs to complete a unit of his output.

**Job description.** The listing of the job's title, tasks, duties, working conditions, reporting relationships and supervisory responsibilities involved in a job. It is the one product of job analysis.

**Job description index (JDI).** A standardized and widely used measure of job satisfaction. This index emphasizes on various facets of satisfaction such as pay, supervision, coworkers, promotions and work itself.

**Job design.** A process of organizing the tasks, duties and responsibilities into a productive unit of work required to perform a specific job. It defined the way the work will be performed and the tasks which will be required in a specific job.

**Job engineering.** The focusing on the tasks to be performed, methods or techniques to be used, layout of the workplace, workflows among the employees, interdependences among the people and the machines and the performance standards. Usually, the experts take the help of time and motion studies to determine the required time for all these individual tasks and the movements needed to perform them efficiently.

**Job enlargement.** A process of expanding/increasing the number of tasks or activities performed by an employee in a specific job. Expansion of a job's duties.

**Job enrichment.** A process of redesigning the jobs in a manner that involves adding more motivators to a specific job in order to make it more rewarding. It increases the opportunities for the employees to experience feelings of growth, achievement, recognition and responsibility. It puts all the specialized tasks back together so that one individual is now responsible for producing a whole product or service.

**Job evaluation.** A process of determining the relative worth of each job in the organisation. It establishes the salary differentials in the organisation.

**Job experience.** All the tasks, duties, demands, problems, relationships and other features which the employees face in their jobs.

**Job factor.** A specific requirement of a job which provides a base for hiring employees and setting wage rates like physical and mental demands, education and experience required, responsibilities, etc.

**Job fragmentation.** The splitting up of an existing job and divide or distribute it among other jobs in the organisation. In other words, it creates a new series of smaller jobs in the organisation.

**Job grading.** The grouping of various jobs in the organisation into grades or classes (which usually carry equal wage scales) on the basis of similarity in the associated responsibility and other requirements.

**Job hazard analysis technique.** A technique of breaking down each job into the basic elements and each of these is rated for its potential for injury or harm. This is done for the identification of potential problems related to the safety.

**Job hierarchy.** The listing of jobs in the order of their significance/importance to the organisation, from the highest to the lowest one.

**Job incumbents.** The people who hold the jobs.

**Job induction.** *See induction*.

**Job instruction training (JIT).** The testing of each job's necessary steps in a proper sequence along with key points (if any) to provide step-by-step training to the workers.

**Job involvement.** The degree to which employees identify themselves with their jobs in the organisation.

**Job mobility.** The readiness of the workers to change their job especially if change in job requires geographical relocation.

**Job posting system.** A system in which a firm announces/publishes job openings to all its employees (by listing the qualifications, pay rates and work schedules) on a bulletin board or in a company's newsletter.

**Job production.** The manufacturing of an article as per a customer's particular order or specification.

**Job redesign.** A process of changing the manner by which work is performed or the tasks in an existing job.

**Job related interview.** An interview in which the interviewer ask a series of job-related questions which focus on the relevant past job-related behaviour.

**Job rotation.** A process that systematically move or shift an employee from one job to another in order to enhance team performance. It is a training technique that broadens employees' experience and prepares the person for an enhanced role in the organisation.

**Job satisfaction.** A positive emotional state (or pleasurable feeling) that results from evaluating one's job experience.

**Job sharing.** A concept of work arrangement that allows two or more workers to share a single full-time job by dividing the job's responsibilities, hours and benefits among themselves.

**Job shop.** The functional organisation whose departments are organised around specific types of operations or equipments like assembly, drilling and forging.

**Job simplification.** *See work simplification*.

**Job specification.** A list of minimum human characteristics or requirements such as knowledge, education, skills, abilities, personality, etc. that a person must have in order to perform a job successfully.

**Job standardization.** The setting or establishment of prescribed ways or methods of doing an operation.

**Job structure.** The relative salaries of the jobs in an organisation.

**Job time.** The time of completing all the elements of a job.

**Job title.** The official name of a particular job in organisation. For example, the human resource manager.

**Job transition.** A process of moving from one job to another job, may be within the same organisation or between different organisations.

**Jobbing.** A process that involves making of small number of products that requires high levels of skills.

**Jobless.** The people who are unemployed or without any jobs.

**Join.** To become a member of an organisation or to start working as an employee of an organisation.

**Joint consultation.** A procedure of promoting mutual understanding and a common purpose between employees and employers.

**Joint consultative committee.** A committee set up for promoting the joint consultations among labour and management.

**Joint councils.** The consultative bodies comprising representatives of employers and employees. Their functions may range from merely advising the management to decision-making on some issues.

**Joint venture.** Any form of association among business firms which implies that the collaboration is for more than a transitory period. This includes contract manufacturing, licensing/franchising agreements and sharing of management and ownership in an enterprise.

**Judge.** A person who take decisions in legal matters or cases.

**Judgment.** The legal decision passed by a judge.

**Judgment sampling.** A type of non-random sampling in which the choice of sample items depends exclusively on the judgment of the researcher.

**Junior.** A person lower in authority or rank in an organisation.

**Junior level management.** The managers who are relatively lower in the hierarchy of an organisation as they are lower in authority or in age.

**Just.** Means the fair and reasonable.

**Just cause.** The reasonable justification for taking an employment-related actions or decisions. It is about fairness in disciplinary action.

**Just-in-time management.** A management system that produces and delivers the finished products just in time to be sold, sub-assemblies just in time to be assembled into finished products, fabricated parts just in time to go into the sub-assemblies and purchase materials just in time to be transformed into the fabricated parts.

# K

**Key jobs.** These are benchmark jobs which are used in pay/wage surveys and which are common to most of the organisations. These jobs have relatively stable content.

**Key-person assurance.** An insurance policy of life of key employee of the organisation, usually a senior manager or executive or director whose death would be a big loss to the organisation. In case of death of key man or woman, then the insurance company would pay the benefit to the organisation.

**Key personnel.** An individual who is of very importance or whose presence is very significant to a business.

**Key result area.** A main area of grouping of activities and their results which are important to an enterprise's success. Also known as **key task analysis.**

**Kinetograms.** A photographic record that displays the real (actual) path travelled by a limb or other parts of the body while performing a given activity or operation.

**Knock off.** To complete work.

**Know-how.** The knowledge of a specific area or field.

**Knowledge-based pay.** A compensation system that pays the employees on the basis of the jobs they can do. This considers the employees specific talent which can be successfully applied to a variety of situations and tasks. Also known as **skills-based pay.**

**Knowledge-based trust.** One of the types of trust in organisational relationships in which the trust is based on the behavioural predictability which comes from a history of interaction. It relies on the information about someone in order to understand them well enough so as to be able to accurately predict their behaviour.

**Knowledge of results.** A process of providing feedback to employees regarding their performance.

**Knowledge worker.** The intellectual workers who can transform information into a product or service.

**KSAs.** Abbreviation for knowledge, skills and abilities, which are required to do a job successfully.

# L

**Labour contract.** A product of collective bargaining which spells out the terms and conditions of employment and also the work rules which affect employees in the organisation.

**Labour cost.** An organisation's expenditure on the wages or salaries paid to the all direct and indirect employees involved in the production of goods or services.

**Labour court.** A court set up under Industrial Disputes Act, 1947*, by the appropriate government* for the adjudication of industrial disputes relating to any matters specified in the second schedule of this act. Matters include application and interpretation of standing orders, discharge or dismissal of workmen, withdrawal of any customary concession, illegality of a strike or lock-out, etc.

**Labour demand.** The number of workers the organisation would require in the future.

**Labour force population.** All the individuals who would be available for the selection purpose if all the possible recruitment methods (for example, internet, newspaper advertisements, employment exchange, etc.) are used.

**Labour intensive industry.** A type of industry that requires a very large number of workers or which consumes large workforce.

**Labour law.** The body of laws which deal with the employment and non-employment, working conditions, industrial relations, wages, labour welfare and social security of industrially employed persons.

**Labour management relations.** A common term used for the relationship (formal and informal) between the employer and his workforce.

**Labour market.** The external supply pool from which the employers attract their employees for their organisations.

**Labour relations specialist.** An expert, usually a member of the Human Resource Department, who has good knowledge about labour relations, provides advice to the top management on labour relations strategy and can represent the employer's interests to a union. He helps in resolving grievances and participates in negotiations with union regarding changes in the labour contract.

**Labour relations strategy.** An organisations's overall plan for dealing with its trade union.

**Labour saving.** A type of work that requires less labour or workers.

**Labour supply.** The availability of employees with the required skills which an organisation might demand.

**Labour turnover.** *See employee turnover.*

**Labour union.** *See trade union.*

**Landrum-griffin act, 1959.** A U.S. act which protects the union members from the possible wrong doing on the part of their unions.

**Lateral flow of communication.** The communication flows between the peers. It is required to achieve cooperation among group members and between work-groups. Also known as **horizontal communication**.

**Lateral integration.** A situation when all the business activities are carried out at the same stage in the production process. Also known as **lateral integration**.

**Law.** The rules/regulations made by the local or state or central government by which a nation is governed.

**Lay-off.** According to section 2 (kkk) of Industrial Disputes Act, 1947*, this refers to the failure, refusal or inability of an employer to give employment to a workman (a) whose name is borne on the rolls of his establishment, and (b) who has not been retrenched. Reasons for refusal may be (i) shortage of raw materials or power, (ii) breakdown of machinery, (iii) accumulation of stocks, and (iv) any natural calamity.

**Leader.** An individual who directs or manage others (i.e., his followers).

**Leader-member exchange (LMX) theory.** A leadership theory which states that the leaders create in-groups and out-groups and the subordinates with in-group states are trusted, have higher performance ratings, less turnover, greater job satisfaction and are more likely to receive special privileges. Out-group followers get less of the leaders time, fewer of the preferred rewards and have leader-follower relations based on formal authority interactions.

**Leader-member relations.** One of the dimensions of Fiedler contingency model, which means the degree of confidence, respect and trust subordinates have in their leaders.

**Leader-participation model.** A leadership theory which relates to the leadership behaviour and the participation in decision-making. It provides a sequential set of rules that should be followed in order to determine the form and the amount of participative decision-making in different situations. This model, developed by Victor Vroom and Phillip Yetton, was a decision tree incorporating 7 contingencies and 5 alternative leadership styles.

**Leaderless group discussion.** A type of exercise used in assessment center* in which a team of 5 to 8 employees is assigned a problem and they must work together to solve it within certain time period. The problem may be assembling a product or nominating a subordinate for a prestigious award in the company.

**Leadership.** The ability to influence a group toward the accomplishment of goals.

**Leading indicator.** An objective measure which accurately predicts the future labour demand.

**Learner control.** The ability of the trainees to learn actively through exercises, self-pacing, conversations with other trainees and experts and exploring links to other materials.

**Learning.** Any relatively permanent change in an individual's behaviour which occurs as a result of experience.

**Learning organisation.** An organisation in which the employees attempts to learn continuously/constantly about new things (techniques, methods, etc.) and apply this in order to improve product or service quality.

**Least preferred co-worker (LPC) questionnaire.** A tool/instrument which measures whether a person is task or relationship oriented. Fred Fiedler created this in order to find out a person's basic leadership style. LPC questionnaire consists of sets of 16 contrasting adjectives (like efficient-inefficient, supportive-hostile, pleasant-unpleasant, open-guarded) on a scale of 1 to 8.

**Leave.** The legal permission to be away from the work.

**Legal.** As per the law.

**Legislature.** One of the institutions of the total political environment which is the law-making body. Also known as parliament at the central level and assembly at the state level.

**Leisure.** Free time i.e., off from work and other official duties.

**Leniency.** A tendency of not being strict while dealing with the subordinates.

**Liability.** Being responsible or liable as per law.

**Liaison.** Communicating or providing information to other interested parties, for example, workers, outsiders, trade union, etc.

**License.** An official document that allows person to do something.

**Lifelong learning.** The continuous upgradation of employees' skills and abilities in the organisation. An organisation provides continuing learning starting from the basic remedial skills to the advanced decision-making skills throughout the workers' careers.

**Lightening strike.** The sudden strike by workers or their union.

**Line authority.** Authority exerted by a manager by directing the activities of employees in his own department. For example, authority exerted by a human resource manager in Human Resource Department.

**Line and staff.** They represent specialization of managerial functions. The line functions are responsible for the organisational goals and objectives, whereas the staff functions help the line function in achieving these goals and objectives.

**Line management.** Employees or managerial persons who have a direct responsibility for attaining goals and objectives of an organisation.

**Line manager.** A manager who is authorized to direct the work of his subordinates in the organisation. He is responsible for attaining the organisation's goals and objectives. He is involved directly in producing the organisation's products or services.

**Literacy.** The mastery of the basic skills (i.e., abilities of writing, reading, speaking, arithmetic).

**Livelihood.** An activity by which an individual earns money/income to support his and his dependants' life.

**Living wage.** A wage that must provide not merely for the bare essentials of life such as food, clothing and shelter, but for a condition of frugal comfort like protection against ill health, education for children, a measure of insurance against life's important misfortunes like old age. Living wage is higher than fair which itself is higher than minimum wage.

**Loading.** The assigning of work to the workers or machines.

**Local.** A specific nearby area.

**Lock-out.** According to section 2(e) of Industrial Disputes Act, 1947*, it means the temporary closing of a place of employment, or suspension of the work, or the refusal by an employer to continue to employ any number of persons employed by him. For lock-out, the essentials include (i) temporary closing of place of employment, (ii) elements of demands due to which employment is closed, and (iii) intention to re-employ the employees in case they accept the demands.

**Lock-out/tag-out regulations.** It means the mechanics and trade persons should be provided with locks and tags to be used to make an equipment imperative for some adjustment or repair in order to prevent accidental start-up of the defective machinery.

**Locus of control.** A degree to which a person believe he is master of his own fate.

**Long range/term planning.** The planning about various activities or operations of an organisation in long run (usually 5 to 10 years).

**Long-term orientation.** A Geert Hofstede's cultural dimension that emphasizes persistence, future and value thrift. It emphasizes future as opposed to the short-term values that focus on the present and the past.

**Loophole.** Some weakness or defect in the set rules and regulations.

**Lottery method.** A method of taking a random sample in which all the items of the population are named or numbered on the separate slips of a paper of identical size and shape. Then these slips are folded, mixed and put up in a container. Finally, a blindfold selection is made of the number of slips needed to constitute the desired sample. Selection of items depends purely on chance.

**Low-context cultures.** The cultures which rely heavily on the words to convey meaning during communication. Spoken or written words are more important than body language or formal titles. This culture is prevalent in North America and Europe.

**Lower-order needs.** The needs which are predominantly satisfied externally. These are physiological and safety needs.

**LPC.** Abbreviation for Least Preferred Co-Worker questionnaire*.

**LSI.** Abbreviation for Lump Sum Increase*.

**Lump sum amount.** An amount paid at a single point of time. For example, on retirement, an employee usually receive a lump sum amount in addition to regular pension.

**Lump sum increase.** A pay increase method in which an employee receives one-time payment of all or a part of the yearly pay increase.

# M

**Machiavellianism**. A personality characteristic which refers to the degree to which a person is pragmatic and maintains emotional distance. It is named after Niccolo Machiavelli, who wrote on the topic 'how to gain and use power'.

**Machinery.** Under Factories Act, 1948*, it includes prime movers, transmission machinery and all other applicances, whereby power is generated, transformed, transmitted or applied.

**Macroenvironment.** The outer environment of an organisation which creates factors that affect an organisation's performance and profits. For example, technological environment, political and legal environment, social and cultural environment, demographic environment, economic environment, etc.

**Mail survey.** A survey in which the respondents are contacted with the help of postal or courier mail service (or through e-mail these days).

**Maintain.** To keep something in a good and satisfactory condition.

**Maintenance.** A function of human resource management* which means sustaining and improving the already established conditions. It is concerned with the establishment of proper health, medical and safety measures.

**Maintenance of membership.** A union rule that requires the employees, who choose to join union, must remain its members for a certain period of time (like the length of the union contract).

**Majority.** A larger group out of the total.

**Maladjustment.** A situation when individual is not happily adjusted/ adapted to his surrounding environment.

**Malcolm baldrige national quality award (MBNQA).** An American award which a U.S. company can receive as the highest level of national recognition for quality. This is established to promote quality awareness and to publicize the successful quality strategies.

**Mall intercept interviewing.** A type of interviewing in which various shoppers in the shopping malls are intercepted and interviewed face-to-face.

**Managed care plan.** A plan which include those approaches which monitor and reduce the medical costs by using restrictions and market system alternatives. It emphasizes preventive care, prices negotiated with physicians and hospital and use of specific providers who will charge lesser rates.

**Management.** 1. The art and science of running an organisation i.e., planning, organizing, staffing, directing, co-ordinating and controlling the work of others in order to achieve the individual, organisational and societal goals and objectives. 2. All the people involved in running or managing an organisation.

**Management appraisal.** The assessment of effectiveness of managers regarding their performance in the organisation.

**Management assessment center.** A simulation exercise in which the management candidates are required to perform some realistic tasks and they are scored on the basis of their performance. Typical simulation exercises include the leaderless group discussion, management games, objective tests, interviews, in-basket and individual presentations.

**Management audit.** A review or evaluation of the management of an organisation usually carried out by an independent firm of management consultants who are expert in this.

**Management buy-in.** The acquisition of an organisation by a team of managers who are specially formed for this purpose.

**Management buyout.** A situation when the management of an organisation attempts to make a bid in order to own it, either wholly or in part, by buying out the shareholders.

**Management by crisis.** A management style in which crash programmes are set up in order to deal with the problems as they arise in an enterprise.

**Management by exception.** A management style in which the managers intervene only when their employees or subordinates fail to meet the required performance standards. The idea is to reduce the load on managers, their entry is only required when it is absolutely necessary otherwise they are free for other important tasks.

**Management by objectives (MBO).** A goal oriented approach in which the supervisor and his workers set specific measurable goals together and then periodically reviewing the progress made.

**Management by wandering around (MBWA).** A management style in which senior executives or managers collect information along with motivating their staff by wandering around the plant. They spend their time by listening to the problems and suggestions.

**Management consultant.** An expert who is usually hired by an organisation in order to provide advise on the improvement of the organisation's efficiency and profitability. The independent experts usually provide a detailed report by giving their recommendations and suggestions.

**Management contracting.** An arrangement in which one firm (usually a domestic company) supplies the management knowhow to another firm (usually a foreign company) which provides the capital in order to create a joint venture*.

**Management development.** Improving the present or future managerial performance by imparting knowledge, increasing skills and abilities or changing attitudes.

**Management game.** A management development technique which divide trainees into 5 to 6 groups who compete with each other by making decisions in simulated market situations. For example, making decisions such as how much to produce, how much to spend on advertisement, etc.

**Management information system (MIS).** A system in an organisation which provides the managers with the facts and figures they require for proper interpretation and decision-making.

**Management inventories.** Audits of managers in the organisation.

**Management of diversity.** A process of creating a conducive environment in the organisation which integrates the nontraditional employees (i.e., woman and minorities) into the workforce and using their diversity to the organisation's competitive advantage. Also known as **managing diversity**.

**Management position description questionnaire. (MPDQ).** A technique of job analysis which consists of a structured questionnaire containing 208 items. These items relate to managerial responsibilities, demands, restrictions and various other position characteristics.

**Management process.** This refers to the five basic functions of management, i.e., planning, organizing, staffing, directing and controlling.

**Management rights.** The rights of the employer to run, direct and control its business and also retain any profits that come from its business. It includes the rights to recruit, promote, discipline and discharge workers.

**Management science.** An approach to decision-making which is based on the scientific method that makes an extensive use of quantitative analysis. Its technique includes linear and goal programming, network and inventory models, simulation, decision analysis, waiting line and markov process models, etc.

**Management service.** Any kind of service in an organisation that intends to help the management in performing its function more effectively.

**Management style.** An approach which a manager adopts in dealing with other people at workplace and specifically while exercising his authority.

**Manager.** An individual who achieve company's goals and objectives through the other people. He is incharge of other employees in the firm and is responsible for the correct and timely completion of the tasks or actions which promotes his unit's successful performance.

**Managerial grid.** A two-dimensional view of leadership style developed by Blake and Mouton which is based on the styles (or axis) of concern for people (y-axis) and concern for production (x-axis). This leadership grid has total nine possible positions along each axis thus creates 81 different leadership styles.

**Managerial judgment.** One of the simplest demand forecasting technique in which managers judge about the future demand of the personnel. Experienced managers who are well-acquainted with the requirements of jobs like workload, ability of employees, future capability, etc. discuss together and reach at the figure of demand of labour. After this estimation, the lower level managers submit their requirement to the higher level managers for consideration and revision, if necessary.

**Managing agent.** Any person appointed or acting as the representative of another person for the purpose of carrying on such other person's business or trade, but it does not include an individual manager subordinate to an employer.

**Managing director.** A director of an organisation who is responsible for routine running of the organisation.

**Mandated benefits.** All those benefits which the employers in U.S. must provide to their employees by law.

**Mandatory bargaining items.** All those items over which bargaining is mandatory under the law. These are those items (for example, over-time pay, pension, etc.) that a party must bargain even if these were introduced by the another party.

**Man-hour.** The total amount of work done/performed by one man/person in one hour.

**Man-machine chart.** A chart which displays the relationship between a machine and work of its operator.

**Manpower planning.** *See human resource planning*.

**Manufacturing process.** According to section 2(k) of Factories Act, 1948*, it means any process for (i) making, altering, repairing, finishing, oiling, washing or adapting any article or substance with a view to its use, sale, transport, delivery or disposal, or (ii) pumping oil, water, sewage or any other substance, or (iii) generating, transforming or transmitting power, or (iv) composing types for printing, printing by letter press, lithography, photo gravure or any other similar process or book binding, or (v) constructing, reconstructing, repairing, refitting, finishing, breaking up ships or vessels, or (vi) preserving or storing any article in cold storage.

**Marginal employee.** An employee who is performing at a minimum acceptable level due to lack of ability and/or motivation to do/perform well, and this is not due to lack of good working conditions.

**Marginal functions.** All those duties which are part of a job but are incidental to the main purpose and nature of a job in the organisation.

**Marginal tax rate.** The percentage of the additional earnings which goes to the taxes.

**Marital status.** A condition of being unmarried or married.

**Market line.** A line that shows the relationship between the job value (which is determined by job evaluation points) and the wage survey rates.

**Masculinity-femininity dimension.** One of the Geert Hofstede's cultural dimensions which describes division of the roles between the sexes within a society. Masculine cultures (like those of Japan, Germany) stress performance, success and competition, whereas Feminine cultures (like those of Norway, Sweden) emphasize putting relationships before money, preserving environment and help others.

**Maslow's hierarchy of needs theory.** *See hierarchy of needs theory.*

**Mass interview.** A situation when a panel of experts interviews several candidates simultaneously.

**Massed practice.** An individual performing all of the practice at once.

**Master.** A skilled employee.

**Master strategy.** *See grand strategy.*

**Maternity benefit.** A benefit provided to women workers in case of confinement or miscarriage, or sickness arising out of pregnancy, confinement, premature birth of a child or miscarriage.

**Maternity benefit act, 1961.** An act that regulates the employment of women in certain establishments for certain periods before and after child-birth and to provide for maternity benefit* and certain other benefits.

**Maturity curve.** A curve which shows the relationship between the experience and pay rates.

**MBNQA.** Abbreviation for Malcolm Baldrige National Quality Award*.

**MBO.** Abbreviation for Management by Objectives*.

**MBWA.** Abbreviation for Management by Walking or Wandering Around*.

**McClelland's theory of needs.** *See achievement motivation theory.*

**MD.** Abbreviation for Managing Director*.

**Mean.** An average of all values or numbers.

**Measured day work.** A wage assessment method in which a daily production target is established and a daily wage agreed on that basis.

**Mechanical observation.** The observation tools and techniques that involve mechanical observers either in association or in place of human observers. For example, eye-camera, psychogalvanometer, etc.

**Mechanistic organisation.** An organisation structure with very clearly specified roles of all employees along with clear definitions of their rights and obligations. Certainty of the environment is essential for this kind of organisational structure.

**Median.** The middle value in a distribution. It is just the 50th percentile value below which the 50 per cent of the values of a sample falls. In other words, it just divide the observation into two halves.

**Mediation.** In an industrial dispute*, the intervention by an independent third party who enables the two sides to reach on an agreement. In other words, it is a third-party intervention used to overcome an impasse* in collective bargaining* in which a neutral third party assists the two parties to reach an agreement.

**Medical benefit.** This refers to the provision of medical treatment, under Employees State Insurance Act, 1948*, to an insured person and/or a member of his family (where such medical benefit has been extended to family). This benefit may be given either in the form of out-patient treatment and attendance in a hospital / dispensary / clinic or by visits to the home of insured person or treatment as in-patient in a hospital.

**Medical benefit council.** A council constituted to advise the employees state insurance corporation* on the medical side of its operations.

**Medical test.** A test that reveals the physical fitness of a candidate.

**Medicare.** A part of U.S. social security program which provides health insurance coverage for people aged 65 and above.

**Mega-option grants.** An incentive in which an employee (usually CEO) gets bigger, enormous upfront grants, from the firm, in lieu of the annual grants.

**Membership group.** A group to which an individual belong and the group has direct influence on his behaviour.

**Mentor.** An experienced senior employee who helps in guiding, advising and developing a less experienced junior employee. He acts as a role model for the juniors.

**Mentoring.** A development oriented formal or informal program in which senior employees help junior ones or peers by guiding, sharing contacts, role modeling and providing career advise.

**Merit bonus.** The bonus paid to an employee as a result of his good performance.

**Merit increase grid.** A grid which combines a worker's performance rating with his position in a salary range in order to determine the size and frequency of his salary/pay increase.

**Merit pay.** An increase in the salary which usually becomes a part of the employee's basic pay. Generally given once a year. Also known as **merit raise**.

**Merrick differential piece rate system.** An incentive system developed by D.V. Merrick. This system introduces three piece rates and made the lowest piece rate equal to the ordinary rate which becomes the base piece rates. The rates introduced by Merrick are the following:

| Sl. No. | Output (%age of t.ask) | Piece rate wage |
|---|---|---|
| 1. | Less than 83% | Basic piece rate |
| 2. | From 83% to 100% | 110% of basic piece rate |
| 3. | Over 100% | 120% of basic piece rate |

For the potentially high producer, this plan is a good incentive system. This plan pays a production bonus at 10 per cent of the basic rate to the workers when they reach 83 per cent task and further 10 per cent bonus on reaching over 100 per cent.

**Michigan model of HRM.** A hard model of HRM* which emphasizes that employees are resources in the same way as any other business resource. They must be obtained (a) as cheaply as possible, (b) used sparingly and (c) developed and exploited as much as possible.

**Microenvironment.** The environment near to an organisation that affects its working. For example, organisation's suppliers, customers, competitors, etc.

**Middle management.** A term usually applied to describe those managers who are responsible for the execution and interpretation of policies.

**Migrant worker.** A worker who comes from the other region, state or country to work. The main reason of migration is good wages.

**Minimum wage.** A wage that provides not merely for the bare sustenance of life, but also for the preservation of the efficiency of an employee.

**Minimum wages act, 1948.** An act that makes provision for the statutory fixation of minimum rates of wages in a number of industries where the labour is not organised and sweated labour is most prevalent. It secures the welfare of the workers in a competitive market by fixing the minimum rates of wages in certain employments.

**Minor.** An individual who has not attained the age of eighteen years.

**Minority.** Small number of people out of the total.

**MIS.** Abbreviation for Management Information System*.

**Miscarriage.** The expulsion of the contents of a pregnant uterus at any period prior to or during the 26 weeks of pregnancy. Law does not include any miscarriage, the causing of which is punishable under the Indian Penal Code, 1860.

**Misconduct.** The bad behaviour or action.

**Misrepresentation.** Any wrong or untrue statement of fact which is intentionally made by one party to the another during negotiations to persuade other party to enter into the contract.

**Mistake.** Any misunderstanding on a statement or on matters of a fact and also sometimes on matters of law.

**MNC.** Abbreviation for Multinational Corporation*.

**Mobility of labour.** The willingness on the part of workers to move from one place or region or state or country to another.

**Mobility premiums.** A lump sum payment given to an employee for moving/shifting from one task/ assignment to another one.

**Mode.** A value in a series of observations which occurs with the greatest frequency. For example, the mode of the series 2, 5, 7, 5, 6, 8, 1, 5, would be 5, as this value occurs more frequently than any of the others.

**Model.** A simplified representation of real world phenomenon.

**Monthly wages.** The amount of wages which is deemed to be payable for a month's service.

**Moonlighting.** When a person have two jobs at a time, one of them on full time basis (day time job) and another a part-time job in the evening.

**Morale.** It describes the overall attitudes of a person or group collectively towards all the aspects of their work—the job, organisations, peers, working conditions, etc. In other words, it is the summation of attitudes of employees.

**Motion.** A proposal put for discussion before a meeting. Generally, all the members to a meeting receives a notice of motion so as they can consider it before the actual meeting. When the majority members pass the motion then it becomes a resolution.

**Motivation.** An individual's desire to do the best in his job.

**Motivation-hygiene theory.** A theory which state that intrinsic factors are related to job satisfaction and the extrinsic factors are related with dissatisfaction.

**Motivation to learn.** The desire or willingness of an employee to learn (especially during a training program).

**Motive.** Which persuades human action.

**Multimedia technology.** A type of electronic communication which integrates text, video and voice, all of which are encoded digitally and can be transported on the fibre optic networks. This makes it possible to interact with employees video images around the world.

**Multinational corporation (MNC).** An organisation having its operating units located in the foreign countries.

**Multi-stage sampling.** *See cluster sampling*.

**Multiple choice question.** A question on a questionnaire which carries a list of answers (usually 4 or 5) and the respondent is required to select one answer out of these.

**Multiple correlation.** A statistical tool which deal with situations that involve three or more variables. Coefficient of multiple linear correlation is represented by $R_1$. For example $R_{1,2,3,4}$ means coefficient of multiple linear correlation between $X_1$, on one hand and $X_2$, $X_3$ and $X_4$ on the other.

**Multiple intelligence.** Intelligence which covers the subparts like emotional, cognitive, cultural and social intelligence.

**Multivariate analysis.** A statistical analysis that involve three or more variables. For example, multiple correlation*, multiple regression*, etc.

**Mutual welfare.** Those welfare activities which are undertaken by the workers themselves through the platform of their trade unions. This include reading room, indoor games, etc.

# N

**National economy.** A fundamental principle of labour legislation that takes into consideration the general economic situation of the country. The state of the national economy is a significant factor in influencing labour legislation of a nation.

**National emergency strike.** A strike which might impact the national economy significantly.

**National labour relations act, 1935.** A U.S. act that protect employees' right to form and join unions and to engage in activities like collective bargaining*, strikes* and picketing*. This has banned certain types of unfair practices. *See Wagner Act also.*

**National labour relations board (NLRB).** An independent agency created by the Wagner Act* in U.S. to administer U.S. labour law. It is required to investigate unfair labour practice charges and to administer certification elections (i.e., secret ballot elections which determines whether or not a firm's employees want to be represented by a union).

**National tribunal.** A tribunal set up under Industrial Disputes Act, 1947*, by central government, for the adjudication of industrial disputes which, in the opinion of the central government, involve questions of the national importance or are of such a nature that industrial establishments situated in more than one state are likely to be affected by or interested in such disputes. It shall consist of only one person to be appointed by the central government.

**Natural justice.** The minimum standards of justice to be maintained by a court while resolving a dispute. For example, right to be heard given to each party, impartiality in settling the dispute, etc.

**Natural wastage.** A method of managing an organisation's activities and decisions without making its employees redundant, only relies on the retirements, resignations, quits or deaths. This is the most suitable way of reducing workforce, when lot of time is available.

**Need for achievement.** A drive to excel, strive to succeed and achieve in relation to a set of standards. People with a high need for achievement have a intense desire for success and an equally intense fear of failure. They set moderately difficult goals (but achievable) for themselves.

**Need for affiliation.** The desire for friendly and close interpersonal relationships. People with a high need for affiliation oftenly derive pleasure from being loved and tend to avoid the pain of being rejected by a social group.

**Need for power.** The need to make other people behave in a way that they would not have behaved otherwise. Individuals with a high need for power have a great concern for exercising influence and control.

**Needs assessment.** A process which is used to determine if the training is necessary.

**Negative affectivity.** A dispositional dimension which reflects the pervasive individual differences in satisfaction with any and/or all aspects of life. Individuals who are high in negative affecting tend to focus more on the negative aspects of themselves and others. They report higher levels of aversive (opposed) mood states like nervousness, anger, fear, guilt and disgust across all contexts (i.e. work and nonwork).

**Negligent hiring.** Hiring an employee with questionable or objectionable background (history of illegal or violent behaviour) without taking proper precautions or conducting background checks.

**Negligent training.** When an employer fails to train an employee adequately or properly and the employee subsequently harms a third party.

**Negotiate.** To discuss in order to arrive at mutually acceptable terms for an agreement or contract.

**Nepotism.** A practice of favouring relatives or kins over the others at the workplace.

**Network.** A combination of desk top computers (PCs), computer terminals and mainframes which share access to the databases and a method (way/mean) to transmit information throughout the system.

**New entrants.** 1. The people who are looking for the work for first time. For example, college and university leavers. 2. Those firms who are entering in an industry for the first time, may be newly established companies or already established but in other fields.

**New technologies.** The current applications and use of procedures, methods, equipment and knowledge which have not been previously used.

**NLRB.** Abbreviation for National Labour Relations Board*.

**No-strike agreement.** An agreement between labour and management according to which the workers or their trade unions promise to never resort to strike in an organisation. Also known as **non-strike clause**.

**Noise.** The distraction or interference which interferes with or disturbs the communication process.

**Nominal group technique.** A group decision-making method in which individual members of the group meet face-to-face in order to pool their judgments in a systematic but independent manner. All members are physically present, just like in a traditional committee meeting but they operate independently. They present their ideas independently on the problem.

**Nomination.** In life insurance policy, the person to whom the proceeds of the policy should be paid, this is specified by the policyholder in the document.

**Non-compete agreement.** An agreement which prohibits a person who leaves the firm from competing with the employer in the same line of business for a specified or limited period of time.

**Non-contributory plan.** A pension plan in which an employer provides all the funds for the pension benefits.

**Nondirective interview.** An interview in which the interviewer asks questions which are developed from the answers to the previous questions.

**Non-domiciled.** In international human resource management* (IHRM), an individual whose country of domicile is not the same as where he resides for tax calculations.

**Non-executive director.** A company's director who do not have any day-to-day responsibilities within the company.

**Nonexempt employee.** A U.S. employee who is covered by the provisions of the Fair Labor Standards Act* (FLSA), 1938. *See FLSA, 1938.*

**Nonkey jobs.** The jobs which are unique to a firm and cannot be directly valued and/or compared through the use of market/wage survey like key jobs (benchmark jobs*).

**Non-personal communication channel.** A channel of communication which carries messages without personal contact like TV, radio, etc.

**Non-probability sampling methods.** The sampling methods which do not provide every item of the universe with a known chance (or probability) of being included in the sample.

**Non-sampling error.** An error arising at the stage of observation or ascertainment and the processing of the data (for example, tabulation error).

**Normal retirement age.** A person's age when he retires, usually in between 58 to 65 years of age.

**Norming stage.** A stage in group development in which close relationships develop and the group demonstrates cohesiveness.

**Norms.** The acceptable standards of behaviour within a group which are shared by group's all members.

**Norris-laguardia act, 1932**. A U.S. act that encourages union activity and guarantees each employee the right to bargain collectively free from any interference, coercion or restraint.

**Notice.** A written official piece of information.

**Notice of motion.** *See motion.*

**Notification.** An act of informing someone regarding some matter.

# O

**Objectives.** Aims or purposes for which a company is set up and works. They indicates the destination of an organisation.

**Observation.** A method of collecting job data in which the analyst observes the jobholder actually performing the job and then records the key job characteristics from observation. Direct observation is good in case where the job is of routine nature and consists of mainly observable physical ability, for example, job of mechanic, draftsman, etc.

**Obsolescence.** A situation when a machine or equipment is no longer required or becomes outdated.

**Obstruct.** To hinder or to stop someone from progressing. For example, obstruction of inspector under Factories Act, 1948* is a punishable act.

**OCB.** Abbreviation for Organisation Citizenship Behaviour*.

**Occupation.** A group of jobs which are similar as to kind of work and are found throughout the industry or the entire nation. In other words, a group of jobs with common characteristics.

**Occupational diseases.** The certain diseases which are inherent in some occupations. Contracting of occupational diseases is deemed to be an injury by accident within the meaning of section 3 of the Workmen's Compensation Act, 1923*.

**Occupational hazard.** A risk of illness or accident at the workplace. This risk is specifically related with the nature of one's occupation.

**Occupational illness.** Any disease or ailment due to the exposure to the environmental factors associated with the employment.

**Occupational pension.** The pension which a person receives due to his retirement from a specific occupation.

**Occupational safety and health act, 1970 (OSHA).** A U.S. act which requires employers to provide safe and healthful working environment and comply with the specific occupational health and safety standards. Also, he has to maintain the records of occupational injuries and illness.

**Occupier.** An individual who has the ultimate control over the affairs of the factory. He may occupies a factory either by himself or by his agent. He may be an owner, a lessee or a mere licensee, but he must have the right to occupy the property and dictate the terms of management.

**OD.** Abbreviation for Organisational Development*.

**OFCCP.** Abbreviation for Office of Federal Contract Compliance Programs*.

**Off-line.** When the computer equipment is not usable as it is not connected to a computer or internet.

**Off-the-job training.** A type of training in which workers are given training away from their job or workplace. For example, in a training center, classroom, etc.

**Off-the-peg research.** A type of research which uses the existing data for research purposes rather than having a fresh investigation of the case.

**Offence.** An act which is against the law.

**Office bearer.** An individual who hold an office or who is a member of official membership.

**Office of federal contract compliance programs (OFCCP).** A U.S. agency which is responsible for monitoring and implementing the laws and executive orders which apply to the federal government and its contractors.

**Officer.** An individual who acts in his official capacity in an organisation. The officers includes directors, executives, managers, auditors, etc.

**Official strike.** A type of strike which takes place on the instructions (or on the orders) of a trade union.

**Offshoring.** A special case of outsourcing in which the jobs are moved or exported from one country to another. Generally, it includes exporting jobs from the developed nations like U.S. to less developed nations like India, China and Brazil. Major reason for this is labour costs.

**Ohio state studies.** The research conducted at Ohio State University in the late 1940s that attempts to identify the independent dimensions of leader behaviour. The researchers identified two categories which substantially accounted for most of the leadership behaviour described by employees, i.e., initiating structure and consideration.

**Old boy's network.** An informal social network, in the organisation, of male managers and executives which typically excludes women and minorities. Women are hindered by lack of access to the network and access to this is considered as a significant factor (for example, to know inside gossip, CEO's interest in a new product or service, an employee's imminent transfer) in career.

**Ombudsman.** A person who otherwise lies outside the normal chain of command but acts as a problem solver for both the employees and the employer.

**Omnibus questionnaire.** A type of questionnaire that includes questions on numerous different topics.

**On-line.** When a computer equipment is connected to computer or the internet.

**On-line focus group.** A type of research on internet in which the respondents attend a virtual focus group meeting held on a website. Especially useful when all the participants are at different locations.

**On-the-job training.** Training based on the concept of learning by doing. A person learns a job while working on it.

**Open door policy.** A policy adopted by a manager or by management in which unlimited and unscheduled access is provided to all employees.

**Open-ended question.** A question on a questionnaire in which the respondent is required to provide his answer in his own words, instead of yes or no.

**Open shop.** A union security clause in which the employees will decide whether or not to join the union and those who join the union must pay dues.

**Open system.** A system which is affected by the outside influences and it is also able to affect other systems. *Compare it with closed system.*

**Operant conditioning.** A theory of learning that explain a type of conditioning in which the desired voluntary behaviour leads to a reward or prevents a punishment.

**Operation job card.** A card on which a worker writes the details of a specific task along with the time taken to finish it. Usually used in work studies.

**Operation research.** *See management science.*

**Opinion surveys.** Questionnaires used to ask employees regularly their opinions about the organisation, management and work life.

**Opportunity to perform.** Opportunities given to trainees to use (or apply) training content on the job so that they maintain their learned capabilities (knowledge, skills, behaviour) from the training program.

**Oppose.** To vote against something or someone.

**Oral communication.** Communication with the help of spoken words instead of written words.

**Order.** The arrangement of things and the placement of the people in the organisation.

**Organic organisation.** An organisation with no clearly specified roles, as people interact with each other so the definitions of tasks redefined and less emphasis on authority. In this, the communication is both vertical as well as lateral and the decision-making is decentralized. Uncertainty of external environment exists. *Compare it with mechanistic organisation.*

**Organisation.** 1. In context of organisation structure, it means the network of relationships among individuals and positions in an organisation. 2. In the sense of a process, it means determining, arranging, grouping and assigning the activities to be performed for the achievement of goals and objectives of the organisation.

**Organisation-centered career planning.** A career planning that concentrates on the jobs and on the identification of career paths which would provide for the logical progression of people between the jobs in an organisation.

**Organisation chart.** A chart which shows the various positions in the organisation and the formal relationships among them. It displays graphically important aspects of an enterprise including its major functions, their respective relationship, the channels of supervision and the relative authority of each employee who is in charge of each respective function or area.

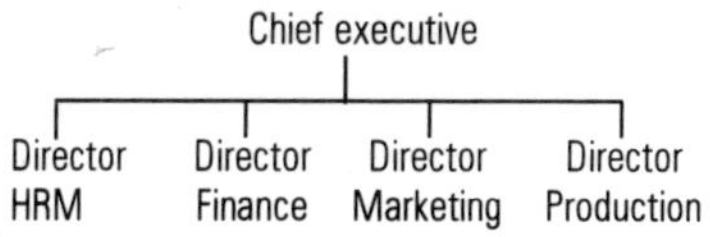

**Organisational analysis**. A sub-part of need assessment of training which considers the context in which training will occur. It determines the business appropriateness of training i.e., a firm's business strategy, top management support for training and resources available for training.

**Organisational audit.** Audit of all operations of an organisation.

**Organisational behaviour.** A field that study the impact that individuals, groups and structure have on behaviour within organisations in order to apply such knowledge for improving an organisation's effectiveness.

**Organisational challenges.** The problems or challenges internal to an organisation.

**Organisational citizenship behaviour (OCB).** The discretionary behaviour which is not a part of an employee's formal job requirements in the organisation, however it promotes effective functioning of the organisation. For example, employee's performance beyond expectations, etc.

**Organisational climate.** The relatively enduring characteristics that remain stable over a period of time, and which describe an organisation and distinguishes one organisation from the others, and also they influence people's behaviour in the organisation.

**Organisational commitment.** The degree to which an employee identifies with a specific organisation and its goals and objectives and also wishes to maintain its membership.

**Organisational culture.** The common perception and beliefs shared by the members of an organisation. These beliefs operate unconsciously and exercises a significant influence on the attitudes, behaviour and performance of members of the organisation.

**Organisational design.** The manner or the way in which the managers build the organisational goals and objectives. It clearly specified the tasks, duties and responsibilities of individuals and departments.

**Organisational development (OD).** A systematic, integrated and planned method of changing the beliefs, values and attitudes of employees so that they can improve the organisation. It is a comprehensive and long-range, usually takes 3 to 5 years.

**Organisational development intervention.** Techniques which attempts to change/modify employee's behaviour, values and attitudes.

**Organisational psychology.** *See industrial psychology*.

**Organisational socialisation.** A process of transforming new employees into effective members of the organisation. It includes providing information (like company's history, goals, work performance) to employees.

**Organisational structure.** A network of relationships among individuals and positions in an organisation. A skeleton framework of an enterprise.

**Organisational theory.** A study of the structure, design and the process of decision-making in organisations.

**Organising.** A process of establishing harmonious authority-responsibility relationships among the members of the organisation.

**Orientation.** A planned introduction of the new employees to their jobs, colleagues and the organisation. Informing new employees about the job, co-workers and what is expected from them in the job.

**OSHA.** Abbreviation for Occupational Safety and Health Act, 1970*.

**Out of court.** Mutual settlement arrived between the two parties privately without continuing their case in the court.

**Outcome appraisal instrument.** An appraisal tool which asks managers to assess the results achieved by the employees like number of products produced or total sales.

**Outcome fairness.** The judgment which individuals make with respect to the outcomes received relative to the outcomes received by the other individuals with whom they identify (referent others).

**Outplacement assistance.** A systematic program in which the firms help or counsel their departing/ terminated/displaced employees in finding new jobs by providing them training in job-search skills. It helps the employees to manage transition from one job to another. Also known as **outplacement counselling**.

**Output.** The work done, quantity produced, results of the work performed, etc.

**Outside director.** An individual who is a member of board of directors in an organisation but not an employee in that organisation and has no responsibilities. These kind of directors are appointed due to their rich experience and expert knowledge in that particular field.

**Outsourcing.** Allowing outside vendors (who are more efficient in doing the similar work) to provide their services. Subcontracting work to an outside firm which specialize in doing that kind of work.

**Outwork.** The work carried out by a person in his own home or some other places rather than in the organisation's premises.

**Outworker.** An individual who works from his home for an organisation.

**Overlearning.** A process in which the trainees continue to practice even if they have been able to perform the objectives so many times. It increases the length of time a trainee will retain the knowledge, skill and behaviour and becomes more comfortable.

**Overmanning.** A situation in which an organisation have more number of workers than required. Also known as **overstaffed**.

**Overtime.** The time (in hours) an employee work beyond the normal working time (usually 9:00 a.m. to 5:00 p.m.) in an organisation.

**Overtime ban.** A situation when the employees refuse to work overtime.

**Owner.** A person who owns something. For example, the owner of a factory.

# P

**PA.** Abbreviation for Personal Assistant*.

**Paid time-off plan.** A plan which includes all the sick leave, vacation time and holidays into a total number of hours or days which an employee can take off with pay.

**Paired comparison method.** A performance appraisal method in which the appraiser compares each employee (for every trait like quality of work, quantity of work) with every other employee, one at a time. Number of comparisons may be calculated as $\frac{N(N-1)}{2}$ where N stands for the number of employees to be compared.

**Panel interview.** An interview in which several interviewers interview the candidate/applicant at the same time.

**PAQ.** Abbreviation for Position Analysis Questionnaire*.

**Parameter.** A single value obtained to describe in summary the key characteristics about a population.

**Parent country.** A country in which an organisation's corporate headquarter is located.

**Parent country nationals (PCNs).** Those employees who born and employed in a parent country*.

**Part-time worker.** A worker who do not work for the full/whole working day. For example just 4 hours per day.

**Partial disablement.** Any disablement that reduces the earning capacity of a workman as a result of some accident. It may be temporary or permanent.

**Participative management.** The use of joint decision-making. A process through which the subordinates share decision-making power with their immediate superiors.

**Paternalistic theory.** A theory of labour welfare according to which an industrialist or employer holds the total industrial estate, properties and profits accruing from them in trust and the labour welfare work depends entirely on the initiative of the top management. This theory is also known as **trusteeship theory** and was strongly advocated by Mahatma Gandhi.

**Paternity leave.** A short duration leave (usually 5 to 10 days) given to a male employee when his wife delivers a baby.

**Path-goal theory.** A contingency theory of leadership which states that it is leader's job to assist his followers in achieving their goals and provide the essential direction and/or support in order to ensure that their goals are compatible with the overall objectives of the group or organisation. Based on the belief that the effective leaders clarify the path (reduce bottlenecks) of their followers to attain their work goals. This theory was developed by Robert House.

**Pattern bargaining.** A process in which a trade union gains a new and superior entitlement from one employer and later on uses this agreement as a precedent in order to demand the almost same or still more superior one from the other employers.

**Pay.** The wage or the salary given to an employee for his regular work in the organisation.

**Pay-as-you-earn (PAYE).** A mean of collecting tax on employee's wages and salaries. As per this scheme, the employer collects the tax from his employees on the payments made to them. The employer then remits the collected tax with the concerned authority.

**Pay compression.** A situation in which the pay differences among individuals with different levels of experience and performance becomes small. This type of situation is prevalent in many occupations like information technology industry.

**Pay day.** The day of a month on which employees are given their pay.

**Pay equity.** The similarity in the pay for all the jobs requiring comparable levels of knowledge, skill and abilities (KSAs*) even if the actual duties differ significantly.

**Pay for performance system.** A system that rewards employees on the basis of their relative performance in order to attract, retain and motivate high performers.

**Pay freeze.** A situation when salaries of employees are held or freezed at their existing levels. It is a difficult situation and it cannot be maintained in long run.

**Pay grade.** Groups of jobs, of approximately equal difficulty, which are paid within the same pay range.

**Pay incentive.** A component of total employee compensation which is designed to reward employees for their good performance.

**Pay level.** The average pay including the salaries and bonuses of the jobs in a company.

**Pay-off.** The last payment made to terminate a contractual relationship.

**Pay policy.** An organisation's decision to pay above, below or at going rate for its job. An organisation decides whether to lead, leg or pay the market rate.

**Pay policy line.** It is a mathematical expression which describes the relationship between a job's pay and its job evaluation points.

**Pay ranges.** A series of steps (or levels) within a pay grade, which are generally based upon years of service.

**Pay satisfaction questionnaire (PSQ).** A questionnaire that measure the specific dimensions of pay satisfaction of employees like pay levels, pay structure, benefits and pay raises. It provides a more detailed view of exactly what aspects of pay are least or most satisfying.

**Pay slip.** A document given to an employee in order to explain him how his salary is calculated. It shows the gross salary, its various components (for example, house rent allowance, dearness allowance, dearness pay, etc.) along with the deductions from gross salary (for example, income tax, group insurance, etc.) if any and finally, the net salary of an employee.

**Pay structure.** The relative pay of different jobs (i.e. the job structure) and how much they are paid (i.e. the pay level).

**Pay survey.** Collection of the data on the compensation rates for the employees performing similar jobs in other companies.

**PAYE.** Abbreviation for Pay-As-You-Earn*.

**Payee.** An individual or an organisation to be paid.

**Payer.** An individual or an organisation who makes a payment.

**Payment by results.** *See pay for performance system.*

**Payment in kind.** A payment which is not made in cash but in goods or services. For example, staff prices on company's products, discounts on airfares for Air India's employees.

**Payment of bonus act, 1965.** An act that provides for the payment of bonus to the persons employed in certain establishments. The scheme of the act is four-dimensional, i.e., (a) to impose statutory liability upon an employer of every establishment covered under this act to pay bonus to its employees; (b) to define the principle of payment of bonus according to prescribed formula; (c) to provide for the payment of minimum and maximum bonus and also, linking the payment of bonus with the scheme of 'set-off' and 'set-on'; and (d) finally to provide the machinery for the enforcement of the liability for the payment of bonus.

**Payment of gratuity act, 1972.** An act that provides for a scheme of compulsory payment of gratuity by the managements of factories, mines, oil-fields, plantations, ports, railway companies, shops and other establishments employing 10 or more persons drawing monthly wages not exceeding Rs. 3,500 in the event of retirement, superannuation, resignation and death or disablement due to disease or accident. This act is a progressive social security measure.

**Payment of wages act, 1936.** An act that ensures the payment of wages, to the persons employed in industry, at regular intervals without any unauthorized deductions. This act provides against the irregularities in the payment of wages and unauthorized deductions by the employers.

**Payroll.** A list of names of all employees of an organisation. Oftenly used to describe total amount paid to all employees in an organisation.

**PBGC.** Abbreviation for Pension Benefit Guaranty Corporation*.

**PDA.** Abbreviation for Pregnancy Discrimination Act*.

**Peer.** A person who is working at the same level/hierarchy or who is of same age.

**Peer review.** A performance appraisal method in which employees at the same level in the organisation appraise or rate one another.

**Peer review panel.** An internal committee of employees to which employees are allowed (by employer) to appeal disciplinary actions. The panel hear appeals and makes decisions or recommendations.

**Peer trainers.** An approach to cross-functional training in which high-performing employees help the employees in developing skills in another area of operation. Peer trainers must be patient and motivated to teach others. *See Cross-functional training.*

**Pegging wages.** When government fixes the wages at existing levels in order to prevent them rising during the period of inflation.

**Penalty.** Punishment for any undesirable act or omission of any act. It may in the form of imprisonment or some fine or both.

**Pension.** Regular payment or money received by a person after his retirement as a part of a pension scheme.

**Pension benefit guarantee corporation (PBGC).** A U.S. government agency established under ERISA* that requires employers to pay for plan termination insurance which guarantees the payment of retirement benefits to employees even if the plan terminates before they retire. Plan may terminate due to poor investment decisions or the firm has gone out of business.

**Pension fund.** A fund generated by persons who contributes under a pension scheme.

**Pension plan.** A plan which provides a fixed sum to employees when they reach a predetermined retirement age or when they can no longer work due to their disability.

**Pensionable earnings.** A part of an employees' salary which is used to assess his final pension. Usually, the bonuses, commissions and over-times are excluded from this.

**Per capita income.** An average income of a group which is calculated by dividing the total income of the group by its total number of members.

**Perception.** A process by which people organise and interpret their sensory impressions in order to give a meaning to their environment.

**Performance.** An employee's notable achievement or which he do in the organisation.

**Performance appraisal.** A process of evaluating and measuring how well employees perform their jobs as compared to a set of standards and communicating the obtained information to employees. Identification of performance deficiency (if any) and also determining whether the deficiency should be corrected by training or by some other means (like transferring the employee).

**Performance consulting.** A process that links the training needs for enhancing organisational performance. In this, a trainer (may be internal or external to the organisation) and the organisational client work together to raise workplace performance in support of organisational goals. Performance consulting approach compares the desired and actual organisational results, then desired and actual employee performance and then needs analysis to identify whether there is need of training or a non-training action is required.

**Performance feedback.** A process of providing employees the information regarding their performance effectiveness in the organisation.

**Performance indicators.** The key indicators of an organisation's performance which are monitored in order to ensure its success in long-run. These indicators reflect the organisation's strengths and weaknesses.

**Performance management.** A process of managing all those elements or parts of organisational process (means goal setting, selection and placement of employee, training and development, performance appraisal, compensation, career management) that affect how well employees perform.

**Performance management system.** A system designed not only to manage but also to improve the performance of the workforce of the organisation.

**Performance measures.** The ways in which the performance of an organisation in total or its parts (for example, departments, divisions, sections, etc.) is measured. These measures can be in the form of quantitative or qualitative measures.

**Performance planning and evaluation (PPE) system.** A system that attempts to tie the formal appraisal process to the organisation's strategies, by specifying in the beginning of the evaluation period the types and the levels of performance which must be attained to achieve the strategy. At the end of the evaluation period, the individuals and groups are evaluated on the basis of how closely their actual (or real) performance met the company's performance plan.

**Performance replacement chart.** A chart that shows inside candidate's present performance and promotability for the most important (key) positions. Usually done for the organisation's top positions.

**Performance standards.** The expected levels of performance for employees.

**Performing stage.** A stage of group development when the group is fully functional. Usually this is the last stage in the group development for permanent work groups.

**Perks (perquisites).** The noncash incentives (like company car, first-class air travel, mobile, club membership, security, reserved parking, company plane, etc.) given to company's executives. They keep them happy but seldom linked to business objectives and goals.

**Permanent partial disablement.** Any disablement that reduces the earning capacity of a workman in every employment which he was capable of undertaking at the time of injury.

**Permissive issues.** Those collective bargaining issues which are not mandatory but they relate to certain jobs. For example, benefits for the retired workers and product prices for the employees.

**Persistent unemployment.** A constant type of unemployment, due to lack of jobs.

**Person analysis.** An analysis that helps an organisation to identify who needs training. It involves (a) determining whether the deficiencies in a person's performance results from the lack of knowledge, skill or ability (i.e. a training issue) or from a work-design or motivation problem, (b) then identify who require training and (c) determining the person's readiness for the training.

**Person characteristics.** An employee's knowledge, skills, abilities, attitudes and motivation. These factors influence an employee's performance and learning.

**Person-job fit.** Matching people's knowledge, skills and abilities (KSAs) with the job characteristics.

**Person-organisation fit.** The congruence (i.e. suitability) between the individuals (values, goals, interests, expectations, KSAs) and the organisational factors (objectives, values, cultures, rewards, strategies, structure and management).

**Personal assistant (PA).** A person who is appointed to assist/help a manager or an executive or a director. Usually, he carries more responsibilities than a secretary.

**Personal communication channels.** The channels through which two or more people communicate with each other. For example, with the help of internet, on phone, face to face, etc.

**Personal influence.** The impact of a person's statement on the attitude of another person.

**Personal loan.** A loan given to a person by a bank or any society (for example, cooperative, building, etc.) for some domestic purposes. For example, house construction, purchase of bike or car, etc.

**Personal pension plan.** A plan in which a person can save money in order to have pension on his retirement. Usually, the plan is operated by an insurance company and mostly utilized by those people whose occupation do not provide any pension on retirement.

**Personality tests.** The tests that attempts to measure the basic characteristics of an individual. These tests measure emotional stability, extroversion/introversion, agreeableness, conscientiousness, self-confidence, etc. For example, Thematic Appreciation Test*, Bell Adjustment Inventory, etc.

**Personality traits.** All those enduring characteristics which describe a person's behaviour.

**Personnel.** The people who work for an organisation.

**Personnel department.** A department in an organisation which is concerned about all the aspects related with human resources (personnel) in that organisation like their recruitment, training and development, promotions, transfers, etc.

**Personnel file.** A file maintained for every employee that contains documentation of critical human resource related information like salary history, disciplinary actions and performance appraisals. Access to this file is controlled and limited.

**Personnel management.** The traditional name of human resource management. Its area of operation was limited. For example, just record-keeping, etc. *See HRM**.

**Personnel manager.** A manager* who is incharge of taking care of all aspects related with human resources in the organisation.

**Personnel selection**. *See selection*.

**PESTL analysis.** An analysis of the influence of environment on an organisation. PESTL stands for political, economic, social, technological and legal issues.

**Phased retirement.** A strategy, usually adopted by employers in order to retain the talents of the older employees, in which the employees reduce their workloads, and salary. This approach allow experienced older workers to have more personal flexibility and on the other hand, the organisation retains them for their valuable capabilities.

**Philanthropic theory.** A theory of labour welfare according to which a philanthropist (man with affection for mankind) strives to remove the sufferings of others and promotes their well-being. Under this approach, employers provide crèches, hostels, canteens, good working conditions, etc. to promote workers' well-being.

**Physical ability.** The capacity of an individual to perform the tasks that require strength, stamina, dexterity and other similar characteristics.

**Physical ability tests.** The tests which measure individual abilities like endurance, muscular movement and strength.

**Picketing.** Watching and dissuading the people who go to work during a strike*. Union members, posted at the factory gates, persuade visitors and others not to enter premises.

**Pictogram.** A method of presenting statistical data by the use of attractive and easy to comprehend pictures. The symbols/pictures are self-explanatory. For example, a story about a aeroplane shows clearly aeroplane's picture.

**Pie-diagram.** A method of showing the data in the form of percentage breakdown. For example, government expenditure is shown to be distributed into different heads like defence, agriculture, industry, transport, etc.

**Piece-rate system.** A compensation system in which workers are paid per unit produced. Pay is based upon the number of items produced by each employee in a unit of time (like items per hour or per day).

**Pilot study.** A technique used in research when out of the total sample, first few respondents are interviewed or proposed questionnaire is filled from them, in order to check whether the proposed questionnaire require some sort of revision or not.

**Placement.** Fitting an individual to the right job. Determination of the job to which an accepted candidate is to be assigned and his assignment to that job.

**Plaintiff.** An individual who starts/took a legal action against someone.

**Plan.** An outcome of the planning* process. A blueprint for the decided future course of action. Plans includes programs, budgets, schedules, procedures, rules, objectives, etc.

**Planning.** A primary function of management that involves determining in advance, the objectives and goals and selecting a course of action to achieve them. It is deciding in advance what is to be done, when and where it is to be done, how and by whom it is to be done.

**Plant.** A large factory* or machinery.

**Plant closing law.** A U.S. worker adjustment and retraining notification act that requires notifying workers when an employer decided to close its facility.

**PM.** Abbreviation for Preventative Maintenance*.

**PMTS.** Abbreviation for Predetermined Motion-Time Standards*.

**Point method.** An analytical or quantitative method of job evaluation which involves identifying compensable factors, each having several degrees and also the degree to which each of these factors is present on the job. Common factors in use are (a) skills, (b) responsibility, (c) effort, and (d) working conditions.

**Police theory.** A theory of labour welfare which is based on the assumption that without policing i.e., compulsion the employers do not provide even the minimum facilities for their employees. So, state assumes the role of a policeman and compels the employees to provide the various welfare facilities to their employees.

**Policy.** A broad statement that provide guidance in decision-making (at lower levels of management). General statements of understandings which guides thinking in decision-making of subordinates.

**Political science.** A science that studies the behaviour of individuals and groups in a political environment.

**Polycentric approach.** An approach to manage international operations in which subsidiaries employ more host country nationals are used in the organisation.

**Polygraph.** The lie detector.

**Polygraph tests.** A test designed to ensure the accuracy of the information provided in the applications.

**Population.** *See universe*.

**Population hypotheses.** The assumptions made by a researcher about some characteristic of a population under study.

**Population pyramid.** A diagram which shows the distribution of a population by age group.

**Portable benefits (portability).** The employees benefits (usually the retirement benefits) which stay with the employee as he moves from one organisation to another. These benefits will always be the employee's property. A pension plan characteristic which allows employees to move their pension benefits from one employer to another.

**Position.** A group of tasks assigned to one individual. In an organisation, there are as many positions as there are personnel.

**Position analysis questionnaire (PAQ).** A questionnaire which is used to collect the quantifiable data concerning the duties and responsibilities of various jobs. It is a very structured job analysis questionnaire. It consists of 194 items (like written materials, visual displays) each of which represents a key element that may or may not play a significant role in the job.

**Position audit.** The assessment of an organisation's present situation i.e., its strengths and weaknesses of an organisation and opportunities and threats from the environment it faces.

**Position power.** One of the dimensions of Fielder contingency model which means the degree of influence derived from one's formal structural position in the organisation (it includes the power variables i.e., power to hire, fire, discipline, promotions and salary raises).

**Position replacement card.** A card developed for each position in the organisation in order to show the possible replacement candidates and their present performance qualifications, promotion potential and training.

**Positive discipline.** A discipline procedure which encourages or motivates the employees to monitor their own behaviours and also assume the responsibility for their actions.

**Power.** In context with Factories Act, 1948*, it refers to the electrical energy which is mechanically transmitted and is not generated by the human or animal agency.

**Power bargaining.** A union-management relation in which the management accepts the trade union and each side tries to gain the advantage from the other.

**Power distance.** A Geert Hofstede's cultural dimension which describe the extent to which a society accepts that in organisations and institutions power is distributed unequally. This ranges from relatively equal (i.e., low power distance) to extremely unequal (i.e., high power distance).

**Power styles.** The styles of management in using power to attain its results. Management style affect employees behaviour in an organisation. There are three styles which are recognized, (a) **impression management**. A competitive power style, normally by manipulations, to overcome any move of opposition. (b) **consensus and charismatic power styles**. The first-one uses joint decision making and joint problem-solving and the second one uses manager's personality in order to inspire and motivate its employees to work collectively for a common purpose. These two are the types of collective use of power. (c) **transactional style**. Depending on the decisionmaker this can be either collective or competitive power styles. In order to have any transaction takes place, cooperation is required but this transaction may become very competitive if it requires the use and allocation of the scarce resources.

**PPE.** Abbreviation for Performance Planning and Evaluation*.

**PPOs**. Abbreviation for Preferred Provider Organisations*.

**PR.** Abbreviation for Public Relations*.

**Practice.** To perform regularly the learned task. It involves having the worker demonstrate what he has learned during the training.

**Preautomation analysis.** An analysis which precedes the replacement of a manual system by automation.

**Precincts.** A space enclosed by walls or fences.

**Precoded questionnaire.** A questionnaire which is coded before it is sent to the respondents.

**Predecessor.** A person who holds a position or a job or an office before another person occupies or takes it.

**Predetermined motion-time standards (PMTS).** A work measurement technique which makes use of libraries of pre-established time, for the basic human motions in order to construct the standard times for the jobs or for processes.

**Predictive validation.** A criterion-related validity that attempts to establish a relationship between the applicant's test scores and their eventual job performance.

**Preexisting condition.** A medical condition which was treated while the employee was covered under the former employer's health plan and requires further treatment under a new employer's different health plan.

**Preferred provider organisations (PPOs).** The groups of health care providers that make a contract with the employers, insurance companies or third-party payers to provide a broad set of medical care services at a very reduced fee. PPO's let employees to select providers (such as doctors) from a wide list and see them in their offices and the providers agree to give discounts.

**Pregnancy discrimination act, 1978 (PDA).** A U.S. act that prohibits the employer using pregnancy, childbirth or related medical conditions to discriminate in hiring, promotion, discharge or suspension, or any term or condition of employment.

**Prejudice.** Biasness or ill feelings against someone.

**Preliminary interview.** An introductory interview during selection process which is quite short and just aims at elimination of the obviously unqualified. This is generally done in order to weed out those who do not possess the minimum requirements laid down for the vacancies.

**Premises.** Building with its outbuildings (building separate from the main building).

**Premium.** Money given/paid to the insurance company for providing coverage.

**Premium bonus.** A payment by results method of paying the employees, in this a standard time is established for each unit's production and the bonuses are paid related to the actual time taken by the employee.

**Preretirement counselling.** A formal counselling provided to those employees who are about to retire. This counselling covers the matters like explanation of social security benefits and investment, second careers outside the firm as well as inside the firm, spending usefully leisure time, health matters and psychological counselling.

**Presentation.** A verbal report usually supported by slides, charts or other illustrative material on a specific topic presented to the concerned audience.

**Presentation methods.** Those training methods in which the trainees are the passive recipients of the information. These include traditional classroom instructions, audiovisual techniques and distance learning.

**Pretesting.** Conducting the trial tests of a questionnaire in order to know its suitability for a research project.

**Preventative maintenance (PM).** A way of plant maintenance in which frequent proactive inspection and repair is emphasized to reduce the downtime and to enhance its working life.

**Priestman system.** A bonus system applicable to those workers who work in groups.

**Primacy effect.** It occurs when the rater gives more weight to the information received first.

**Primary data.** Those data which are collected afresh and first-hand and thus happen to be original in character.

**Primary research.** A research method in which data are collected afresh, first-hand and original in character for the particular study or project being conducted.

**Prime mover.** Any engine, motor or any other appliance which generates or provides power.

**Principal.** With reference to the 'agency theory' it means a person (like owner) who attempts to direct the other person's behaviour.

**Principal employer.** The owner or occupier of the factory and includes the managing agent, and legal representative of a deceased owner or occupier and the manager of the factory.

**Principle of 'last come, first go'.** A principle of retrenchment which states that the management should start with the latest recruit or hired and progressively retrench employees higher up in the seniority list.

**Privacy act, 1974.** A. U.S. act that guarantees the privacy of personnel files for employees of the U.S. federal government. It requires federal agencies to allow employees to examine, copy and amend employee information in their personnel file.

**Privilege.** The advantages associated with a specific situation. For example, privileges given to a trade union once it got registered under Trade Union Act, 1926*.

**PRO.** Abbreviation for Public Relation Officer*.

**Proactive human resource management.** *See union substitution*.

**Probability.** An expression of chance of occurrence of an event. It is a number that ranges from 0 to 1, zero stands for an event that cannot occur and one stands for an event that is certain to occur.

**Probability sampling method.** A sampling method in which every item in the universe has a known chance (or probability) of being chosen in the sample.

**Probation.** Testing or trail period for newly inducted employee in an organisation.

**Problem.** A discrepancy between some present state of affairs and some desired state.

**Problem definition.** The first stage in a research which involves a clear definition of the problem to be solved. It also includes the clear cut objectives of the research.

**Problem-solving team.** A group of 5 to 10 employees, usually from the same department, who meet for a few hours each week in order to discuss the various ways of improving efficiency, quality and the work environment.

**Procedural justice.** The perceived fairness of the process used to determine distribution of rewards. It focuses on the methods used to determine the outcomes received.

**Procedure.** A chronological (planned) sequence of steps to be undertaken in order to enforce a policy and to attain an objective. Also, refers to the customary methods of handling the activities.

**Process.** A series or a set sequence of stages or steps which make up an activity.

**Process chart.** A chart that provides a detailed picture of the work flow i.e., the flow of inputs to and outputs from the job under consideration.

**Process reengineering.** Reconsidering how the work can be accomplished and how an organisation can be structured if it has to start all over again.

**Procurement.** It deals with obtaining proper kind and right number of personnel at the right time and at the most economical rates so that organisational goals and objectives could be easily accomplished. Specifically, it is concerned with the subjects like human resource planning, recruitment, selection, orientation and placement.

**Production cells.** Grouping of employees who make/produce the components or the entire products. Any two employees or as many as fifty employees can be grouped into a production cell and each cell has all necessary equipment and machines. It is used in a number of manufacturing operations.

**Production-oriented leader.** One of the dimensions of University of Michigan studies that emphasizes the technical or task aspects of the job. The production-oriental leader's main concern is to attain his group's task and the group members are a mean to that end.

**Productivity.** A measure of how much value individual employees add to the products or services which an organisation produces of the quality and quantity of the work done by taking into consideration the cost of the resources employed.

**Productivity agreement.** An agreement between an employer and a trade union in an organisation that consists of an increase in wages or salaries to be given for a measured increase in the productivity.

**Productivity bargaining.** A type of collective bargaining in which the management offers a salary rise in exchange for changes in working practices of employees that ensures increased productivity. This all leads to productivity agreement*.

**Proficiency.** The competency or skill.

**Proficiency tests.** Tests conducted to assess the skill, competency and technical knowledge of a person.

**Profit-related pay (PRP).** An employee's pay which is related with the profits made by the organisation. The aim behind this scheme is to motivate the workforce and raise their effort and commitment.

**Profit-sharing plan.** An organisation wide program which provides compensation based on some established or set formula designed around the organisation's profitability.

**Programmed learning.** A systematic (step-by-step) self-learning method that involves presenting the questions, problems or facts to the learner; allowing that person to respond and then provide feedback on the accuracy of his answers. Its main advantage is that it reduces the training time. Also known as programmed instruction.

**Progression of withdrawal.** A situation in which the dissatisfied employees enact a set of behaviours in succession in order to avoid their work situation.

**Progressive discipline.** A discipline procedure which uses a series of management interventions (warning steps) that provides employees opportunities to correct their undesirable behaviours before being discharged. Usually, it consists of four steps—verbal warning, written warning, suspension and discharge.

**Projection.** The attribution of one's own characteristics to other people.

**Promotability forecasts.** Decisions made by the managers regarding the advancement potential of their subordinates. This help the organisation to identify individuals who appear to have high advancement potential.

**Promotion.** Advancement to a position of increased responsibility, greater challenge and more authority than the previous job.

**Proportional stratified sampling.** A type of stratified sampling in which the number of items drawn from each strata is proportional to the size of the strata.

**Prospective.** An individual who may be appointed for a job.

**Protean career.** A career which is changing frequently due to both changes in the individual's interests, values and abilities and changes in the work environment.

**Protected class.** People like women and minorities who suffered discrimination in the past and who are given special protection by judicial system.

**Protégé.** The person under the protection of the other person.

**Protest strike.** *See token strike.*

**PRP.** Abbreviation for Profit Related Pay*.

**Psychological contract.** An unwritten (or unstated) agreement that establishes what an employer expects from the employee and *vice versa*.

**Psychological success.** A feeling of pride and accomplishment which comes from achieving the life's goals.

**Psychological tests.** The tests which are designed to measure achievement, mental alertness, aptitude, physical dexterity, etc. These tests are used by organisations as an aid in the selection of prospective candidates.

**Psychologist.** A person who studies the human behaviour.

**Psychology.** A science that attempts to measure and explain the behaviour of human and other animals. It studies and seeks to understand the individual behaviour.

**Psychomotor tests.** A skill-based test which measures a person's dexterity, hand-eye coordination, arm-hand steadiness and other factors. For example, MacQuarie test for mechanical ability measure manual dexterity for assembly-line workers.

**Psychosocial support.** To serve as a role model and a friend, give positive regard and creating an outlet for a protégé to talk/discuss about his fears and anxieties.

**Public.** Any group of individuals, for example, media, public, etc.

**Public relations (PR).** A technique of influencing the public so that they regard a person or a company, etc. in a favourable/good way especially in comparison with their competitors.

**Public relations officer (PRO).** A person in an organisation who deals with the media. He provides information about the organisation in the form of handouts.

**Public relations theory.** A theory of labour welfare in which the labour welfare work is used as a tool of advertisement to project the organisation's good image on the minds of public. It provides an atmosphere of goodwill between the management and labour and also between management and public outside.

**Public utility service.** According to section 2(n) of Industrial Disputes Act, 1947* it refers to: (a) any railway service or any transport service for the carriage of passengers or goods by air, (b) any service in, or in connection with working of any major port or dock, (c) any section of which the safety of establishment or the workmen employed therein depends, (d) any postal, telegraph or telephone service, (e) any system of public conservancy or sanitation and (f) any industry which supplies power, light or water to public*.

**Punctual.** Being on right time at the place.

**Punctuated-equilibrium model.** A temporary group development model that shows the various transitions between inertia and activity, a group goes through. This is an alternative model (for temporary groups with deadlines) in contrast with the five stage group development model (forming, storming, norming, performing and adjourning).

**Punitive damages.** The fines awarded to a plaintiff to punish the defendant.

**Purposive sampling.** *See judgment sampling*.

**Pygmalion effect.** A situation in which one person (for example, a manager) perceives inaccurately a second person (for example, employee) and the resulting expectations cause the second person to behave in ways which are consistent with the original perception. And the result is expectations become reality. For example, if a manager expects employees to perform low or minimum, then they will tend to behave that way and if a manager expects good performance from his employees, then they will not likely to let him down.

# Q

**Qualification.** A legal and formal written proof that recognizes an individual has successfully completed a specific course.

**Qualification inventories.** Records containing data on employee's educational backgrounds, career and development interests, languages, specific skills, performance records, etc., that helps managers in selecting inside (current) employees for promotion. These inventories may be manual or computerized.

**Qualified individuals.** Persons who can carry out the essential functions of the job. They must have the requisite skills, education and experience to do the job.

**Qualitative forecasting techniques.** The techniques used to forecast future trends like demand forecasting for personnel required. Main techniques include are delphi technique and nominal group technique.

**Quality.** The totality (entirety) of the characteristics and features of a product or service which bear on its ability to satisfy the given needs. Quality measures how well a product or service meet the customer needs and expectations.

**Quality circle.** A small group of employees doing similar type of work who voluntarily meet on the regular basis to identify and solve work related problems in order to improve quality and productivity and to minimise the cost. They monitor productivity and quality and suggest/provide solutions to the problems.

**Quality of life.** A Geert Hofstede's cultural dimension which describes the degree to which individuals value relationships and show concern and sensitivity for the welfare of the others.

**Quality of work life.** A measure of how satisfied and safe the employees feel with their jobs. A high quality of work life is related with job satisfaction which results in a strong prediction of absenteeism and employee turnover.

**Quantitative ability.** It is concerned with the accuracy and speed with which an individual can solve the various arithmetic problems.

**Quantitative forecasting techniques.** The techniques used to forecast future trends by making use of historical data. For example, time series analysis, etc.

**Quantity of life.** A Geert Hofstede's cultural dimension which describes the degree to which the values like acquisition of money, material goods, competition and assertiveness prevail.

**Quartile.** It is one of the three points located on a frequency distribution which divides the total into equal quarters.

**Questionnaire.** A list of questions which deal with some specific topic being studied administered to a sample (group of respondents) in order to obtain data for research purpose.

**Questionnaire method of job analysis.** A method of collecting job related data in which the job holders are required to fill a structured questionnaire which are then approved by their supervisors. It contain information like job title, purpose of job and main tasks or duties of the job.

**Queuing theory.** A theory the objective of which is to study how to maintain a balance between waiting time cost and service cost, so that these two costs are minimum.

**Quid pro quo sexual harassment.** Harassment which occurs when sexual favours/activity is required or demanded for keeping or getting a job or employment related benefits in the organisation.

**Quit.** To resign from a job or to leave the organisation.

**Quoram.** The minimum number of people legally required to be present at or before meeting so that it can officially take place.

**Quota sampling.** A type of non-probability sampling in which quotas are set up according to some specified characteristics like different age groups, different income groups, different religious affiliations, etc. Then each interviewer is told to interview a certain number of individuals which constitute his quota. Within a quota, selection of the sample items depends on the personal judgment.

**Quotas/Quota strategy.** An employment strategy (hiring and promotion decisions) which ensures that a certain number of people from a certain protected class (women and minorities) are hired.

# R

**Racism.** The belief in racist (referring to a person's race) ideas or actions.

**Raise.** An increase in pay or salary.

**Random digit dialling.** A technique for conducting telephonic interview by dialling telephone number randomly selected from a telephone directory.

**Random sample.** A sample whose selection process is such that only chance determines which items shall be included in the sample chosen.

**Random sampling.** A sampling technique where each and every unit of population has an equal opportunity of being chosen in the sample. For ensuring the randomness of selection either lottery method may be used or a table of random numbers may be consulted.

**Random variations.** The uncontrollable variations from a planned performance level. Variations may be due to internal factors (inherent in the process) or external factors (natural climate, etc.).

**Range.** A simple method to study dispersion and is defined as the difference between the value of the largest item and the value of the smallest item included in the distribution. Range = Largest item – Smallest item.

**Range spread.** The distance between the minimum and the maximum amounts in a pay grade. Usually, it is larger at the higher levels because of the fact that performance differences are likely to have more impact on the organisation at the higher job levels.

**Rank.** A position in an organisation.

**Rank and file.** The ordinary workers in an organisation or ordinary members of a trade union.

**Rank order.** The ordering of the responses according to their relative frequency of the responses given by the respondents.

**Ranking method.** 1. An oldest and simplest method of performance appraisal in which one employee is compared with all other employees for the purpose of placing them in a simple rank order of worth. It lists all the employees from the highest to lowest in their performance. 2. The simplest method of job evaluation in which a committee evaluates the job description and ranks the jobs in order of their importance or on basis of overall difficulty. No specific job factors are selected and worth of each job is assessed, job-to-job comparison is made and ranks are assigned.

**Rapport.** The friendly relationship between two persons.

**Rate.** The money charged by a person for the time he worked or for the work or pieces he has completed.

**Rate ranges.** Different employees in same job may have different pay rates (in recognization of the difference in employee performance, training, seniority, etc.).

**Rater error or bias.** An error in performance appraisals which shows consistent biases on the part of the rater or evaluator. Error in which rater's prejudices distort the ratings. One of the most prominent rater errors is halo error.

**Ratification.** A stage during the collective bargaining process in which the union members vote to accept the terms of a negotiated informal labour agreement. When the members approve the agreement then it is formalized into a contract.

**Ratio-trend analysis.** A demand forecasting technique for determining future staff requirement in which past ratio are studied and future ratios are forecasted after making some allowances for changes. For example, ratio between sales volume and number of employees required.

**Rational decision-maker.** A person who makes consistent, value-maximizing choices within the specified constraints.

**Rational decision-making model.** A decision-making model which describes how people should behave in order to maximize some outcome.

**Rational management.** A management style which aims at optimizing the input/output ratio with the help of quantitative techniques.

**Rationalisation.** The reorganisation of an organisation in order to raise its efficiency as well as profitability. This process may include closing those units who are simply duplicating each others efforts, merging some support units, etc.

**Readability.** The ability to read or understand the meaning of written material. Difficulty level of the written materials. Lack of it can impede performance and learning in training programs.

**Real wages.** Means the purchasing power of money wages*. Money wages* only express the amount in terms of currency but the real wages gives the actual worth of that amount.

**Realistic job preview (RJP).** A method of creating the appropriate expectations about the job in which realistic (i.e., real or actual) information about the demand's of the job (both attractive and unattractive aspects of job), location, organisation's expectations of the holder and the work environment in the organisation. This information may be presented either to the applicants or to the newly selected employees before they actually start their work.

**Reality shock.** A phenomenon which occurs when a new employee's high job expectations confront (or met) with the reality of a boring and unchallenging job.

**Reasonable accommodation.** An action taken by organisation in order to accommodate the known disabilities of either the applicants or the employees so that the disabled persons enjoy equal employment opportunity. Creating facilities readily accessible to and usable by disabled persons.

**Reasoning ability.** An individual's capacity to find out solutions to numerous diverse problems.

**Recency effect.** An error in which the rater or evaluator gives more weight to the recent events while appraising a person's performance.

**Recruiting yield pyramid.** A method used by employers to calculate the number of applicants they must generate in order to recruit (hire) the required number of new employees. For example, a company knows that it needs 50 new entry-level data entry operators next year. From its experience the company knows the ratio of offers made to actual new hires is 2 to 1 (i.e., about half the persons to whom it makes offers accept them). Also, the company knows that the ratio of candidates interviewed to offers made is 3 to 2, whereas, the ratio of candidates invited for interviews to candidates actually interviewed is about 4 to 3. So, now the company knows that of six leads that come in from all its recruiting efforts, only one applicant gets an interview i.e., a 6 to 1 ratio.

Fig. 1: A recruiting yield pyramid.

*Source*: Gary Dessler, *Human Resource Management*, Pearson Education, Delhi, 2004, p. 98.

**Recruitment.** A process of searching for the prospective employees and stimulating them to apply for the jobs in the company. Generating a pool of qualified candidates for a particular job in the organisation, i.e., the first step in the hiring process.

**Recruitment process outsourcing (RPO).** Outsourcing of hiring-related jobs to the third-party vendors in order to save costs as well as time. It also improves quality of hiring. It allows an human resource manager to focus on other core functions. Also, right hiring is viewed as a most important step toward reducing attrition.

**Red tape.** The rules and regulations that creates large paperwork.

**Red-circled employee.** An employee whose salary is above the range set for the jobs.

**Redeployment.** The movement of employees from one place to another or to give them different jobs to perform.

**Redundancy.** An employee's loss of job as the work is no longer available to him in the organisation. Due to changes in technology, competition, etc., large number of jobs now cease to exist.

**Redundancy payment.** A payment given to a worker who has been dismissed due to redundancy.

**Reengineering.** A fundamental rethinking, review and radical redesign of business work processes in order to make them more efficient and achieve dramatic improvements in the quality of the end product or service. Aim is to achieve improvement in critical measures of performance like quality, service, speed and cost.

**Referee.** An individual appointed by the two parties, in an arbitration process, under a mutual understanding, to settle the dispute between them.

**Reference group.** An important group to which individuals either belong or hope to belong and with whose norms, the individuals are likely to conform.

**Referrals.** Those individuals who prompted to apply for a job by current employees in the organisation. It is a source of recruitment as present employees know both the organisation and his acquaintances (for example, family member/friend) and hopefully would try to do please both.

**Registrar.** A person appointed by a state government to act as a registrar of trade unions for the state. He has the authority to administer the provisions of Trade Union Act, 1926*.

**Regression analysis.** A technique that attempts to establish the nature of relationship between two or more variables and thus provide a mechanism for forecasting.

**Reinforcement.** Individuals tend to repeat those responses which give them some type of positive reward and avoid those actions which are associated with the negative consequences.

**Reinforcement theory.** A theory of motivation which states that behaviour is a function of its consequences.

**Reinstate.** To re-employ the employee in the same job.

**Rejection.** When a person is not selected.

**Relatedness needs.** A core need group under ERG theory* that emphasizes the importance of interpersonal and social relationships. They align with Maslow's social need and the external component of Maslow's esteem classification.

**Relational database.** A database (several data files containing employee information) which stores information in separate files (like tables) and which can be linked by some common elements/ fields like name, identification number or plant location.

**Relative judgment.** A performance appraisal format in which supervisors are required to compare an employee's performance to the performance of other employees doing the same job. Rank order of employees from best to worst is an example of a relative judgment approach.

**Relay.** In a factory*, where work of the same kind is carried out by two or more sets of workers during different periods of the day, then each of such set is known as relay.

**Reliability.** The degree of consistency of the results (or scores) obtained by the same person when retested with the identical or equivalent tests. A test is considered to be reliable if it yields the same result even if a person is tested for the second or third time provide the test and situation remains the same.

**Relieve.** To work at the place of another worker in order to make him relax for some specific duration.

**Religious theory.** A theory of labour welfare which is based upon two aspects, investment and atonement. As per first aspect, any good work is considered as an investment by which both the benefactor and the beneficiary are rewarded. Whereas, the atonement aspect implies that the current disabilities of a person are the result of the sins committed by him earlier. So, he should take up welfare work now to atone or compensate for his sins.

**Relocation.** To shift a specific work or the whole organisation to a new place.

**Remedial transfers.** Transfers made to remedy the situation. These take place if the initial placement of the employee has been faulty, or the employee cannot get along with the department. Then his transfer to a more appropriate job or under a more agreeable supervisor might result in better performance.

**Remuneration.** The compensation or payment given to a person for obtaining his services.

**Reorganisation.** The process of restructuring an organisation.

**Repartriation.** A process of preparation (planning, training and reassignment) of the expatriates (global employees) for return to their home country from their foreign assignment.

**Repetitive work.** A work that involves repeating same task over and again. For example, in case of work simplification.

**Replacement.** The act of putting someone (a worker) or something (machine, equipment, spare part, etc.) in the place of another.

**Representative heuristic.** Estimating the likelihood of an occurrence by drawing analogies (partial likeness between things which are compared) and seeing identical situations in which they don't exist.

**Representative participation.** A practice in which employees participate directly in the organisational decision-making by a small group of representative employees. The aim of this practice is to redistribute power within an organisation, put the labour on a more equal footing with the interests of employers and shareholders.

**Reprimand.** To criticise someone publicly.

**Repurposing.** Directly translating an instructorled, face-to-face training program online. Those online learning that merely repurposes an ineffective training program will remain effective.

**Request for proposal (RFP).** A document which outlines for the potential consultants and vendors the type of service desired, type and number of references needed, number of workers who need to be trained, funds for the project, follow-up process used to determine the level of satisfaction and service, expected completion/finishing date and finally, the date when the proposals must be received by the organisation. RFP helps the company to identify several vendors who meet the criteria and eliminate those outside vendors who cannot provide the needed services.

**Residual unemployment.** In an economy, this represents the total number of people that still remain unemployed even where there is full employment. This mainly include physically or mentally handicapped people.

**Resignation.** An act of leaving a job or giving up a job.

**Resistance to change.** The employees resistance towards any change in the organisation. This may be due to some misunderstanding, lack of full information, job insecurity (from new technologies), etc.

**Responsibility.** The obligation of a person to whom certain tasks and duties has been assigned to perform them to best of his ability. Responsibility arises from authority and cannot be delegated.

**Restricted policy.** An employer's hiring policy which intentionally or unintentionally excludes the members of a protected group.

**Results.** The measurements used in order to determine a training program's pay off for an organisation.

**Retaliation.** The punitive (penalty) actions taken by the managers or employers against those individuals who exercise their legal rights (for example, an employee who file discrimination charges).

**Retention.** The act of retaining or keeping the employees so that they do not leave your organisation for other rival organisations.

**Retirement.** A time at which an individual gives up his work usually between the ages of 58 to 65.

**Retirement pension.** *See pension.*

**Retraining.** Training of employees again in order to suit the changing requirements of a job.

**Retrenchment.** According to section 2(oo) of Industrial Disputes Act, 1947*, it means termination by the employer of the service of a workman for any reason, whatsoever, otherwise than as punishment inflicted by way of disciplinary action. But it does not include: (i) voluntary retirement of an employee; or (ii) retirement of an employee on reaching the age of superannuation.

**Retrenchment strategy.** A business strategy adopted by struggling firms in which they bring reduction in personnel. This strategy is followed in order to survive in competitive environment.

**Return on investment (ROI).** A useful technique of controlling the performance, calculated by dividing the net profits with the total investment in or expenditure for human resource activities.

**Reverse discrimination.** In U.S., it refers to the claims that white males (i.e., non-protected class members) are discriminated due to use of quotas of protected classes in recruiting and hiring.

**RFP.** Abbreviation for Request for Proposal*.

**Right.** The ability (of employees) to engage in a conduct which is protected by law or social sanction, i.e., free from the interference of the other party like employer. For example, workers have a legal right to form a trade union.

**Right-sizing.** A process of reorganising the organisations workforce in order to improve their efficiency. For example, a company may need to right size when there are too many bureaucratic work processes or management layers which add no value to its product or service.

**Right to privacy.** Freedom from unauthorized and unreasonable intrusion into the personal affairs of individuals.

**Right-to-sue letter.** Under U.S. laws, it means a letter issued by EEOC (Equal Employment Opportunity Commission) which notifies a complainant that he has 90 days to file a personal suit in a federal court.

**Right-to-work law.** A U.S. law which makes it illegal within a state, for a union to include a union shop clause in its contract. It prohibits an employee to join union as a condition of obtaining or continuing employment.

**Rings of defense.** An alternative approach to a layoff plan in which organisation hire temporary supplemental employees (oftenly as independent contractors) with the understanding that their work is temporary, they may be laid off at any time.

**RJP.** Abbreviation for Realistic Job Preview*.

**ROI.** Abbreviation for Return on Investment*.

**Role.** A set of expected behaviour patterns in relation to someone who occupies a given position in a social unit. Means what an organisation expects from an employee (i.e. what to do and how to do it).

**Role ambiguity.** The uncertainty about what an organisation expects from an employee in terms of what to do on the job and how to do it.

**Role analysis technique.** A technique which enables a role occupant and other members of the role occupant's role set (coworkers, subordinates, supervisors) to specify and examine their expectations for the role occupant. So, everybody is gathered together, each person prepares his list, all expectations are written out to remove ambiguities.

**Role behaviour.** The behaviour which are required of a person in his role as a jobholder in a social work environment.

**Role conflict.** A situation when an individual is confronted by divergent role expectations.

**Role expectations.** How others believe (or expect) an individual should act in a given situation. For example, role of a judge is viewed as having dignity, role of an umpire in a match is viewed as being neutral and independent person.

**Role identity.** Certain attitudes and key behaviours consistent with a role. For example, when a union member promoted to a supervisory position, his attitude changes from pro-union to pro-management and in case of his demotion (later on in future), he once again adopt his pro-union attitude.

**Role model.** Means any individual who serves or act as an example for others. People tend to emulate his behaviour or actions. This term was introduced by Robert K. Merton.

**Role overload.** A situation or a state in which a lot many expectations or demands are placed on individuals. It can result in dissatisfaction.

**Role perception.** A person's view of how he is supposed to act in a given situation.

**Role-playing.** A training technique in which trainees assume or play roles of specific persons (for example, a manager, a supervisor, a trade union leader) in a realistic management situation.

**Role plays.** A type of exercise used in assessment centres in which a participant takes the role or part of a manager, executive or other employee.

**Role transition.** A process of changing or switching from one role to other role.

**Role underload.** A situation in which a person feels that his role is not big for him to perform.

**Rorschach ink blot test.** It is a projective test in which the subjects are asked to describe what objects and forms they have seen in a series of ink blots on paper.

**Rowan system.** An incentive system developed by Mr. James Rowan in 1898. In this, a standard time and rate per hour are fixed, the bonus is calculated on the basis of the proportion which the time saved bears to the standard time.

$$\text{Bonus} = \frac{\text{Time saved}}{\text{Standard time}} \times \text{Time taken} \times \text{Hourly rate}$$

**RPO.** Abbreviation for Recruitment Process Outsourcing*.

**Rucker incentive plan.** A plan based on the same philosophy as that of **Scanlon plan***, but the bonus computed is based on a more sophisticated basis. The standard is based upon a careful study of accounting records. This plan offers incentives for saving in wide areas (e.g. in production process) rather than only a savings in labour costs under **Scanlon plan***.

**Rule of res judicata.** A rule, enacted in the section II of the Civil Procedure Code, 1908, which is based on the well recognised principle that once a decision is rendered by a competent authority (like labour court, tribunal) on matter in issue between the parties after a full inquiry should not be permitted to be re-agitated.

**Rule of thumb.** The unwritten but generally accepted business practices which are considered practically useful.

**Rules.** Prescribed guidelines for conduct or action that regulates and restrict the behaviour of individuals in the organisation. They specify what should be done or not done in a specific situation. It is a rigid and definite plan leaving no scope for discretion or deviation.

# S

**Sabbatical leave.** A leave of absence from the organisation for developing skills. Usually, employees on sabbatical leave receive full salary and the benefits.

**Sack.** To dismiss a worker from the job.

**Safety.** A measure in which the physical well-being of persons is protected.

**Safety awareness program.** Programs promoted by employers to create awareness about safety measures among employees.

**Safety officer.** A person appointed by state government (where 1000 or more persons are employed, or where in state government's opinion, any manufacturing process is carried on, that involves any risk of bodily injury or any other health hazard to persons employed in a factory) to take care about the safety of the persons employed in the factory.

**Salaried staff.** Employees who get regular fixed payments.

**Salary.** A payment made consistently to employees for working in the organisation.

**Salary compression.** A salary inequity problem in which longer-term employees' salaries are lower than those of employees entering the organisation today. This is caused by inflation as prices go up faster than the firm's salaries and the firm required a policy to handle it.

**Salary structure.** An arrangement of salary within an organisation in a way that employees doing different jobs will get different rates. These rates are based upon job analysis and job evaluation.

**Salary survey.** A survey conducted in order to determine the prevailing wage rates. It includes survey with the help of formal written questionnaire, telephone, interest and newspaper ads.

**Salting.** A practice in which trade unions hire and pay people to apply for the jobs in certain firms. When these people are hired then they begin organizing efforts.

**Sample.** A representative part of the total universe (population or mass) which is selected for the purpose of investigation. A sample should show the characteristics of the population.

**Sample design.** A plan made for the selection and composition of the sample. For example, whether probability sampling (simple random or stratified random or systematic random or cluster sampling) or non-probability sampling (judgment or convenient or quota sampling).

**Sample size.** The number of sampling units chosen or selected from the universe for investigation. Sample size should neither be too large or too small, i.e., it should be of optimum size. Factors considered while deciding on sample size are: size of the universe, degree of accuracy desired, resources available, method of sampling adopted, nature of respondents and homogeneity or heterogeneity of the universe.

**Sampling.** A process of knowing about the population on the basis of a sample* drawn from it. This process involves the three element, (i) selecting a sample, (ii) collecting the information and (iii) making an inference about the population (on the basis of sample).

**Sampling distribution.** Statistical value/values of samples taken for the proposed study. For example, for each sample, mean and standard deviations are calculated. The means of several samples, taken together, with their relative frequencies becomes the sampling distribution.

**Sampling error.** An error arising due to drawing inferences about the universe (population or mass) on the basis of few observations (sampling). When the whole population is surveyed, it is non-existent.

**Sampling frame.** A list of items from which the sample is to be drawn.

**Sanction.** To give permission. For example, leave of an employee is sanctioned by department.

**Sarbanes-Oxley act, 2002**. A U.S. act which sets stricter rules for corporate behaviour (like accounting practices including requiring more open, transparent and consistent disclosure of financial data) and sets heavy fines and imprisonment for noncompliance.

**Satisfaction.** A feeling of being happy. An employee's state of happiness is considered to be an indicator of being satisfied with his job.

**Save-as-you-earn (SAYE).** A technique of making regular savings that carries certain tax privileges. The regular savings may not be necessarily linked to earnings.

**Saving and thrift plan.** A plan in which the employees are required to contribute a portion of their earnings to a fund. Usually, the employees also matches this contribution in whole or in part.

**Savings.** Money withheld from spending, it is saved for future needs.

**SAYE.** Abbreviation for Save-As-You-Earn*.

**Scalar chain.** The chain of command i.e., the chain of superiors ranging from the ultimate authority to the lowest level in the enterprise.

**Scandinavian studies.** Refers to studies conducted by researchers (in Finland and Sweden) who propose a development-oriented leadership behaviour to suit the dynamic business environment. Development-oriented leader seek new idea, value experimentation, generate and implement change.

**Scanlon plan.** A plant-wide incentive plan developed by Joseph Scanlon of the United Steel Workers of America in 1937. It is designed to encourage involvement, cooperation and sharing of benefits. This plan has two major aspects namely (i) adopting a measure for increase the productivity and (ii) sharing the gains accrued from that productivity.

**Scanning.** An act of examining point by point. For example, scanning of an applicant's application form for the job.

**Scatter plot.** A graphical method of showing the relationship between the two variables. For example, in human resource demand forecasting, a graph showing the relationship between the measure of business activity and the company's staffing requirements.

**Schedule.** Time table or sequence for the achievement of a particular work.

**Schedule planning.** Planning about the schedules (affixing time values) to each activity required and to the total project.

**Scheme.** A plan. For example, employees pension scheme.

**Schever system.** A production planning and control system of German that involves the use of specialised wall charts and also, the direct telephonic communication between the factory operators and the production control staff.

**School-to-work programs.** Programs imparting basic skills training and also includes joint training ventures with high school, colleges and universities.

**Scientific management.** A formal, careful and scientific study of the job in order to increase job satisfaction and productivity.

**Score.** The value given to a particular response to a test item.

**Score keeping.** Maintaining a record of all the scores or data for the interested parties.

**Screening.** Examining the applicants in order to know their suitability for the job.

**Script.** Manuscript or written material of a play or program.

**Seaman.** Means any person forming part of the crew of any ship, but it does not include the master of the ship.

**Search.** Looking for new workers or managers for the organisation.

**Season.** A period of time. A year is divided into 4 seasons (parts), these are spring, summer, autumn and winter.

**Season ticket.** A ticket or pass which gave unlimited access to some service for a particular period of time. For example, bus pass of two or four months.

**Seasonal.** A thing which lasts for a season.

**Seasonal factory.** Means a factory* which is engaged for a period not exceeding 7 months in a year. For example, cotton or jute processing, cotton ginning, manufacture of coffee, indigo, rubber, lac, sugar, tea, decortication of groundnuts, etc.

**Seasonal unemployment.** A type of unemployment that occurs during certain times of a year due to the nature of that particular industry. For example, woollen, tourism, construction, etc.

**Seasonality.** Seasonally adjusted figures or the figures which takes into account the seasonal variations.

**Second.** A staff member who is sent to other organisation, for a fixed time period, in order to help and support them.

**Secondary data.** Data which is already collected or which already exist (prior to the initiation of a research study). For example, government publication, journals, magazines, etc.

**Secondary research.** A research method which make use of the data already collected by others. For example, government publications, books, magazines, journals, newspaper or other sources of data.

**Secretarial.** Means the work of a secretary in an organisation.

**Secretary.** A person who helps in organising the work for someone. For example, organising files, documents, etc.

**Secure.** Means safe.

**Security.** Protection of company's facilities and the employees.

**Security audit.** Review of the organisation's security.

**Segment.** A distinguishable part or position of a total system or business activity, i.e., a part which can be clearly identified.

**Select.** Means to choose.

**Selection.** A process of differentiating between candidates in order to identify and hire those with a greater likelihood of success in a job. All the candidates are divided into 2 groups i.e., selected and rejected.

**Selection criterion.** A characteristic which an individual must possess to perform the job successfully.

**Selection error.** An error which arises due to improper selection process in the sampling.

**Selection rate.** The percentage of candidates hired from a given group of applicants.

**Selective attention.** To single out specific objects from many for concentration or focus.

**Selective perception.** A phenomenon in which individuals selectively interpret what they see on the basis of their background, experiences, attitudes and interests.

**Self-actualization.** A drive to become what an individual is capable of becoming. This is the highest order need in the Maslow's hierarchy of needs. This includes growth, self-fulfillment and achieving one's potential.

**Self-administering test.** A test with a complete set of instructions so that a person can give the test himself by going through instruction by instruction.

**Self-appraisal.** A performance appraisal method in which employees rate themselves. An individual's own assessment of his capabilities. Also called as **self-review or self-assessment.**

**Self-confidence.** An individual's confidence about his own ability.

**Self-confident.** Refers to a person who is very confident in his ability.

**Self-directed learning.** A learning program in which workers take full responsibility for all the aspects of learning.

**Self-efficacy.** An individual's belief in his ability to do a task. A person's belief about his or her chances of successfully accomplishing a specific task. People with high self-efficacy have more confidence in their abilities to succeed in a task.

**Self-employed.** Working for yourself and not for any organisation.

**Self-esteem.** Refers to a person's degree of liking or disliking himself.

**Self-fulfilling prophecy.** *See pygmalion effect.*

**Self-image.** A person's own image about himself.

**Self-made man or woman.** An individual who is rich and successful due to his own hardwork and not due to his inherited money or position. For example, Bharti Airtel's Sunil Mittal has been ranked 3rd in Forbes magazine's 20 self-made Asian billionaires list. Sunil Mittal began his first business in 1976 with $ 1,500 borrowed from his father. Later, co-founded Bharti Group with two brothers. Now, their Bharti Airtel is nation's largest mobile phone operator, with more than 50 million customers.

**Self-managed work team.** A group of 10 to 15 employees who are responsible for producing an entire product or a component and also take the responsibilities of supervisor. *Also, see autonomous work team.*

**Self-management.** A learning technique in which individuals are allowed to manage their own behaviour. This makes the role of external environment control less essential.

**Self-monitoring.** A personality trait which measures a person's ability to adapt (or adjust) his behaviour to the external situational factors. Individuals high in self-monitoring can behave differently in different situations.

**Self-selected group.** A group which is selected as a result of their common response to some stimuli or due to their possession of some common identifying characteristic.

**Self-service.** Providing employees online access to information related with human resource issues like compensation, benefits, contracts, training, completing online attitude survey and enrolling them online in various programs.

**Self-serving bias.** The tendency of people to attribute their own successes to the internal factors and put the blame for their failures on the external factors.

**Self-starter.** An individual who can take initiative in a new situation without asking for any instruction for help.

**Semi.** Means half.

**Semi-skilled.** A worker who had little training, not a fully skilled worker.

**Seminar.** A meeting for some discussion on a specific topic of interest.

**Senior.** An employee higher in rank or older in the organisation.

**Senior management.** A term applied to managers higher in the hierarchy of an organisation.

**Senior mentoring program.** A support program, designed to help women employees, in which senior promising women and minority workers nurture their career progress. This program aim to provide help to women workers in handling a family and their career simultaneously successfully.

**Seniority.** The length of service an individual works for an organisation. It is the oldest and very widely used method as a basis of promotion especially in government owned organisations, unionized industrial establishments and educational institutes.

**Sensitivity (T-group) training.** A training method for raising employees' insights into their own behaviour by discussions in groups led by expert trainers. A small group of trainees consisting of 10 to 12 members is formed which meets in an unstructured situation with no set agenda or plan. Main objectives are more openness with each other, increased listening skills, trust, support, tolerance and concern for others.

**Sensory deprivation.** A situation when people are deprived of the usual stimulations which their senses encounter in their day-to-day life.

**Sentence completion test.** A projective test in which subjects are asked to complete the uncompleted sentence i.e., to fill the blanks in sentences.

**Sentiment.** The feeling and instinct.

**Separation.** The last function of human resource management* i.e., return of the person back to the society. It is concerned with retirement, lay-off, outplacement and discharge.

**Separation agreement.** An agreement between an employer and the terminated employee in which this employee agrees not to sue employer in exchange for some specified benefits.

**Serious health condition.** A health condition of a person requiring immediate medical care (residential or hospital). An employer may require an employee to give such certificate from doctor which verifies such illness.

**Settlement.** According to section 2(P) of Industrial Disputes Act, 1947*, it refers to (a) a settlement arrived at in the course of conciliation proceedings, and includes (b) a written agreement between the employer and workmen arrived at otherwise than in the course of conciliation proceeding where such agreement has been signed by the concerned parties and a copy thereof has been sent to an officer authorised in this behalf by the appropriate government and the conciliation officer.

**Settling-in phase.** A phase in the socialization process which occurs when the employees become comfortable with the job demands and the social relationships.

**Severance pay.** This is a one-time payment given by some employees while terminating an employee. It is a security benefit which is offered voluntarily by the employers to those employees who lose their jobs. These employees may receive a lump sum severance payments in case their employment is terminated by the employer (for example, due to outdated technology, less profitable business, etc.).

**Sexual harassment.** Harassment on the basis of sex which aims at interfering with a person's job performance or creating a hostile work environment. Unwanted and sexually directed actions which subject an employee to adverse employment conditions.

**Shake out.** To bring a complete change, for example, by removing the inefficient work or bad performing companies.

**Shamrock team.** A team consisting of core members, resource experts and part-time (or temporary) members as required. Core members' presence provides stability to the team and the inclusion of resource experts and temporary members provides change to the team.

**Shaping behaviour.** A systematic process of reinforcing every successive step which moves a person nearer or closer to the desired response. Managers attempts to mold individuals by guiding their learning in graduated steps.

**Shift.** In a factory*, where work of the same kind is carried out by two or more sets of workers during different periods of the day, then each of such set is known as relay* and each of such periods is called a shift.

**Short-term planning.** Planning for the organisation's various activities for the next one to two years.

**Sick leave.** The leave which provides pay to an employee when he is out of work because of his illness.

**Sickness.** Means a condition that requires medical treatment and attendance and necessitates absence from work on medical grounds.

**Sickness benefit.** A social security benefit which is payable to those employees who could not perform on their jobs due to illness.

**Simple random sampling.** A type of probability sampling in which each and every unit of the population has an equal opportunity of being selected in the sample. Also known as **unrestricted random sampling.**

**Simulated training.** Training of employees on special off-the-job equipment in a simulated environment in order to reduce hazards and cost. For example, pilot training. It allows employees to see the outcomes of their decisions and actions in an artificial environment.

**Simulation.** A process of designing a model of the real system and then conduct the experiments on that model in order to understand the behaviour of the system.

**Sinecure.** A well-paid comfortable job which involves very little work to do.

**Sinedie.** Means an adjournment of an action indefinitely.

**Sitdown strike.** A type of strike in which workers stay at the place of work but refuse to work or leave.

**Situational analysis.** Analysis of past and future situations an organisation facing, in order to know the opportunities and problems.

**Situational factors.** Organisational characteristics which can influence performance negatively or positively. Also known as **system factors.**

**Situational interview.** A structured interview in which candidates are asked questions dealing with specific situations which are likely to arise on the job and to know what he or she is likely to do in that situation.

**Situational leadership theory (SLT).** A contingency theory that focuses on the level of the followers' readiness. It is the followers who accept or reject the leader. It is regardless what the leader does, the effectiveness depends on the actions of his followers. This theory was developed by Paul Hersey and Ken Blanchard.

**Six sigma process.** A process of measuring, analyzing, improving and controlling processes once they have been brought within quality standards or tolerances. The main purpose is to serve customer what he really wants.

**SLT.** Abbreviation for Situational Leadership Theory*.

**Skeleton staff.** The few staff members doing essential work, whereas most of the other workers are away.

**Skill-based pay plan.** A pay program that set pay levels on the basis of skills the employees have. Also known as **competency-based or knowledge-based pay**.

**Skill variety.** The extent to which work requires various different activities for its successful completion. More the skills are involved, the more meaningful the work is.

**Skills inventory.** Audits of non-managers in the organisation. A record of their education, knowledge, skills and abilities.

**Social audit.** The audit of the impact of non-financial aspects of an organisation on the society.

**Social equity.** A fundamental principle of labour legislation that takes into consideration that with the change of circumstances and ideas there may be a need for change in the law. (Labour legislation based on the principle of **social justice*** fixes a definite standard for adoption for the future, taking into consideration of the events and circumstances of the past and present.)

**Social facilitation effect.** A tendency in which the performance either improve or decline in response to the presence of others.

**Social intelligence.** An individual's ability to relate effectively to others.

**Social justice.** A fundamental principle of labour legislation that means an equitable distribution of profits and benefits accruing from the industry between the employers and workers and also affording protection to the workers against the harmful effect to their health, safety and morality.

**Social learning theory.** A theory which states that individuals can learn through observation and direct experience. People learn by watching their parents, teachers, models, peers, TV actors, seniors, bosses, etc.

**Social loafing.** A tendency of individuals to put less effort when working collectively than when working individually.

**Social psychology.** An area that focuses on the influence of people on one another. It blends the concepts of both psychology and sociology.

**Social security.** A protection program provided against the contingencies of modern life like sickness, old age, unemployment, dependency, industrial accidents and invalidism against which a person cannot be expected to protect himself and his family by his own ability. The main aim of social security includes three-fold i.e., compensation, restoration and prevention.

**Social theory.** A theory of labour welfare which emphasizes that an organisation is morally bound to improve the conditions of the society in addition to improving the conditions of its workers.

**Socialization.** A process of orienting new workers to the organisation or the department in which they will be working.

**Socio-technic system.** A system which studies the interaction of people and machines to improve the efficiency.

**Sociology.** An area that studies the people in relation to their fellow human beings. This studies group behaviour in organisations.

**Soft benefits.** Benefits like customer's satisfaction, enhanced quality which are difficult to measure but provide indirect benefits to the organisation.

**Soft goals.** Means goals which tend to be relationship or trait-based. For example, interpersonal skills, leadership styles, etc.

**Spaced practice.** When several practice sessions are spaced over a period of days or hours.

**Span of control.** The total number of subordinates which a manager supervises at workplace.

**Speak up! programs.** Programs which encourage upward communications by allowing employees to express their concerns, questions and complaints about work-related matters.

**Special purpose team.** A team consisting of members from different functional units whose aim is to address specific problems, study the complex issues like improving the quality of a work process, or service, introducing latest technology, etc.

**Specificity.** The extent to which a performance measure provides detailed guidance to the workers regarding what is expected from them and how they can meet these expectations.

**Split-halves method.** A method of determining reliability of a test in which a test is divided into two equivalent halves and the correlation is found for these halves-test. Generally, there is odd-even split of the test.

**Spreadover.** The total period of work of workers in a factory* including the intervals for rest. As per Factories Act, 1948*, spreadover should not be more than 10½ hours in any day. However, chief inspector may increase spreadover up to 12 hours for some specific reasons.

**Stability strategy.** When the business environment is very stable then a company may follow this strategy i.e., strategy of *status quo*. A firm's satisfaction with the present market share and its products.

**Staff employee.** An employee who assists the line employees in the organisation.

**Staff manager.** A manager who advises and assists the line managers in the organisation.

**Staffing.** A process of filling all the positions in the organisation with adequate and qualified personnel. A process of manning the organisation and keeping it manned.

**Stakeholders.** The various interest groups whose interests are tied to the organisation like shareholders, employees, suppliers, customers and the community.

**Standard deviation rule.** A rule used to determine disparate impact*. It uses the difference between the expected representation for minority groups (women, blacks) and the actual representation in order to determine whether the difference between these two values is greater than would occur by chance. For example, if 30 per cent of the applicants were women candidates then one would expect 30 per cent of those hired to be women. However, only 15 per cent were hired.

**Standard hour plan/system.** An incentive system in which an employee is paid a basic hourly rate and also is paid an extra percentage of his base rate for production exceeding standard per hour.

**Standardization.** Consistency or uniformity of the conditions and procedures.

**Standing committee.** A committee constituted from among the members of the E.S.I. corporation* for the general superintendence and control of E.S.I. corporation*. It act as its executive body.

**Statistic.** A single value obtained to describe in summary the main characteristics about a sample.

**Statistical sampling.** Denotes the random selection and probability theory to know the sample size and then evaluate results after using the sample.

**Status.** A socially defined position or rank given to individuals by others.

**Statutory right.** A right protected by certain laws (or based on laws).

**Statutory welfare.** All those employee welfare activities which are undertaken by employers because of legal requirements. For example, welfare facilities provided under the Factories Act, 1948*, Mines Act, 1952, etc.

**Stay-in strike.** A form of strike in which the employees report for the duty but do not work thus preventing the employer from engaging other workers to carry on his business. Also known as **sit-down/tools or pen-down strike.**

**Stereotyping.** Judging an individual on the basis of our perception of the group to which that individual belongs.

**Stipend.** The remuneration given to certain types of employees for their services.

**Stock option.** An employee ownership plan i.e., his right to purchase a said number of shares of a firm stock at today's price at sometime in future.

**Stoppage.** The act of stopping work in the organisation.

**Storming stage.** A stage in group development which is characterized by intragroup conflict.

**Straight piecework plan/system.** An incentive system in which a worker is paid an amount for each item he makes with direct proportionality between results and rewards. In other words, rate per unit of output is fixed and total wages of a worker are arrived at by multiplying total output by the rate per unit.

**Strategic change.** A change in an organisation's mission, vision and strategy.

**Strategic choice.** A company's strategy (ways) of fulfilling its mission and its long-term goals and objectives.

**Strategic congruence.** The extent to which a performance management system elicits work performance which is consistent with the company's goals and strategy. It emphasizes the need for the performance management system to guide the workers in contributing towards company's success.

**Strategic HR choices.** In designing human resources system, the options/choices available with a company.

**Strategic human resource management.** A process of linking human resource management with the strategic objectives and goals/targets of the organisation to enhance organisational performance and to gain competitive advantage against its competitors.

**Strategic human resource planning**. Formulation of human resource strategies and establishing programs to implement them.

**Strategy.** An organisation's long-term plan showing how it is going to balance its internal strengths and weaknesses with its external environment's opportunities and threats in order to maintain a competitive advantage.

**Strategy formulation.** A process of defining the organisation's mission, goals and objectives, its internal strengths and weaknesses and its external opportunities and threats and then deciding on its st ategic direction.

**Strategy implementation.** A process of allocating resources in order to enact the strategy an organisation has selected.

**Stratified random sampling.** A type of probability sampling in which the universe to be sampled is subdivided (i.e., stratified) into groups which are mutually exclusive and include all items in the universe and then a simple random sample is chosen independently from each group.

**Stress.** Means worry or tension.

**Stress interview.** An interview in which the candidate is made uncomfortable by asking a series of often rude questions. This technique is adopted to identify the hypersensitive applicants and to check their high or low tolerance level.

**Strictness/leniency.** A performance appraisal problem which occurs when a supervisor tends to rate all the subordinate either low or high.

**Strike.** According to section 2(q) it refers to (a) a cessation of work by body of persons employed in any industry, or (b) a concerted refusal of any number of persons who are or have been so employed to continue to work or to accept employment, or (c) refusal under a common understanding of any number of such persons to continue to work or to accept employment.

**Strikebound.** An employee who is unable to work due to strike at workplace.

**Strikebreaker.** An employee who keep on working while other employees are on strike at workplace.

**Structural change.** The redesigning or reorganising of an organisation's departmentalization, decision-making process, span of control, reporting relationships and coordination.

**Structural interview.** An interview in which a set of sequence of questions is followed. It is based on a thorough job analysis and in which job-related questions are asked with predetermined answers. Also called as **directive interview.**

**Structural unemployment.** A type of unemployment that results from the changing structure of an industry. This is long-term unemployment.

**Structured sequential interview.** An interview in which the applicant is interviewed sequentially by several interviewers.

**Subordinate.** An individual working at a lower position relative to others.

**Subordinate review.** A performance appraisal method in which employees rate their supervisors.

**Subsistence allowance.** Means remuneration paid to an employee during his suspension period.

**Substitute.** An individual who takes the place of another individual.

**Substance abuse.** Use of the illicit substances or misuse of the controlled substances, drugs and alcohol.

**Succession planning.** A career planning which focus on the supply of suitable successors for the present and future key or senior jobs in the organisation. Preparing persons to fill executive positions.

**Successor.** An individual who takes charge from other person.

**Suggestion system.** A formal method of getting upward communication from workers or their feedback.

**Summary plan description.** In U.S., under Employee Retirement Income Security Act (ERISA)*, it is the reporting requirement of employers to describe this plan's eligibility requirements, funding, risks, etc. within 90 days once a worker has entered this plan.

**Superannuation.** Means retirement of an employee on the attainment of a certain age.

**Supplemental pay benefits.** The benefits for the time not worked like holiday and vacation pay, sick pay and unemployment insurance.

**Supplemental unemployment benefits.** The benefits paid by the organisation as a guaranteed annual income in certain industries where a person is unable to work though no fault of his own. For example, due to reduced work or change of machinery.

**Supply forecasting.** It provides information regarding the ability of the organisation to procure the required number of personnel. This is concerned with the availability of personnel from within and outside an organisation.

**Support group.** A group set up by top management to provide a nurturing climate for diverse employees who otherwise feel violated or let down.

**Support network.** A technique of enhancing transfer of training in which a group of two or more trainees who meet to discuss their progress in using the learned capabilities on the job.

**Survey research.** A technique of surveying employees' attitudes and the use of this data as a basis for problem analysis and action planning.

**Sustainability.** Capability of an organisation to survive in a competitive business environment.

**Sympathetic/sympathy strike.** A strike which takes place when one union stop work in order to express their sympathy (support) with other workers who are on strike.

**Synergy.** The additional value created by combining/joining two individuals, or firms (more return after joining together than their individual contributions).

**Systematic sampling.** A type of probability sampling in which sample is formed by selecting one unit at random and then selecting the additional units at evenly spaced intervals until and unless the sample has been formed.

# T

**Tabulation.** Presentation of the survey data in the form of statistical tables.

**Tactics.** Specific ways of executing a strategy. They have short-term orientation.

**Taft-Hartley act, 1947.** A U.S. act that limited some of the power acquired by unions under National Labor Relations (Wagner) Act*. It prohibited union unfair labour practices, enumerated rights of employees as union members and rights of employers and allow president of U.S. to temporarily bar national emergency strikes.

**Take-home pay.** The amount actually mentioned on a pay cheque. This includes gross salary minus deductions for taxes, contributions for a pension plan, employees welfare funds, etc.

**Talent.** Skill, aptitude and ability of the performers (for example, employees, actors, models).

**Tall organisation.** An organisation which have a number of levels in its hierarchy.

**Tardiness.** Slow, unpunctual, reluctant, unwilling or late.

**Target.** A very specific, clear-cut and quantitative objective*. For example, total sales expected from a salesman in one day. It is a plan stated in a concrete terms.

**Task.** An identifiable and distinct work activity composed of motions.

**Task analysis.** A detailed study of the job to determine what specific skills the job requires. It is used to identify training needs of new employees.

**Task force.** A group of employees brought together to work on a specific task. For example, a special project. After the successful completion of the task, the group is usually disbanded.

**Task group.** An organisationally determined group, comprises of individual working together to complete/finish a job task. For example, individual from different departments working on a common project.

**Task identity.** This is the extent to which a job includes a whole identifiable unit/piece of work which is carried out from start to finish and also which results in a noticeable (visible) outcome.

**Task leader.** A person who directs (leads) a small group of persons (i.e., task force). He tries to maintain their attention on the particular task and ensures that the task is successfully completed.

**Task significance.** Impact the job has on the other persons.

**Task structure.** One of the dimensions of Fiedler contingency model which means the degree to which the job assignment are procedurized (i.e., structured or unstructured).

**TAT.** Abbreviation for Thematic Appreciation Test*.

**Tax.** Payment made by citizens of a nation to the local, state or central government for their services.

**Tax equalisation.** An approach to handle international taxation in case of expatriate's compensation. Under this approach, the organisation withheld an amount equal to the home country tax obligation of the expatriate and pay all the taxes in the host country.

**Tax protection.** An approach to handle international taxation in case of expatriate's compensation. In this case, the employee pays up to the amount of taxes he would pay on his compensation in the home country. The employee is entitled to any windfall received in case total taxes are less in the foreign country than in the home country.

**Taxable income.** Income which is liable to taxation, as per law.

**Taylor's differential piece-rate system.** An incentive system developed by F.W. Taylor in which high rate and a low rate for each job or task is set. For each job standard output and task time are established. If the output of workers is equal to or exceeds the standard, he receives wages at the higher rate to enable him to get the bonus. On the other hand, if the output of the worker is less than the standard, then he receives wages at the lower rate. The standard is determined on the basis of time and motion studies. This plan is basically designed to encourage the especially efficient worker with a higher rate of payment and to penalize the inefficient by a lower rate of payment.

**Taylorism.** The other name for Taylor's scientific management approach.

**TCNs.** Abbreviation for Third Country Nationals*.

**Tea/coffee break.** Break or rest time during the work period (usually of 15 to 30 minutes) in which the employees can have tea or coffee.

**Teaching machine.** A machine, usually a programmed computer, which can be used to teach the employees without the help of any instructor or teacher.

**Team.** A small number of persons (usually ranges from 6 to 18 employees) with complementary skills who work collectively toward common goals and objectives. Also, they hold themselves mutually accountable for the attainment of these goals.

**Team briefing.** A practice of encouraging communication among the team members.

**Team building.** A process of improving effectiveness of teams (like teams of division directors, corporate officers) with the use of consultants and meetings.

**Team incentive plan (group incentive plan).** An incentive plan in which the standards for production are set for a specific group of workers and its members are paid the set incentives when their group exceeds those standards.

**Team interview.** An interview in which the candidates are interviewed by team members with which they will work in the future.

**Team leader training.** The training of the team facilitator or team manager.

**Teamwork.** Group effort of all team members.

**Technic of operations review (TOR).** A method of determining specific unsafe job elements which has led to past accidents. In order to study past accidents it isolate unsafe elements of a job.

**Technical skills.** Means the knowledge and ability in using the techniques, equipment and procedure involved in performing specific tasks.

**Technician.** An individual who is expert in doing industrial work.

**Technique.** The skilled way of performing on a job.

**Technological change.** Changes or modifications in an organisation's work methods used to achieve the tasks.

**Technological unemployment.** A type of unemployment which arises due to technological changes (usually these results in surplus labour).

**Technology.** Application of scientific knowledge to industrial work.

**Telecommunication.** The long distance transmission of signals.

**Telecommunity (teleworking).** A work arrangement which allows employees to work at remote locations, usually at home full-time and maintaining their contact with the office with the help of computer, phone, video displays and fax*.

**Teleconferencing.** Use of audio and video equipments in order to enable people to participate in the meetings and conferences even when they are at a great distance away from the each other and conference location.

**Telephonic interview.** A type of interview in which interview is conducted on telephone. It is suitable where face-to-face interview is not possible or costly or time-consuming.

**Telex.** A teleprinter machine which helps in communicating written messages over international telephone network.

**Temporary employee.** An employee whose services are hired on a short-term basis only between six months to one year.

**Temporary partial disablement.** Means any disablement that reduces the earning capacity of a workman in any employment in which he was engaged at the time of accident which resulted in such disablement.

**Ten C model of HRM.** A pragmatic model that guides human resource managers in crafting an organisation's specific HRM* strategy. The model suggests ten essential principles (of a sound HRM* programe) these are: comprehensiveness, credibility, communication, cost effectiveness, creativity, coherence, competence, control, change and commitment.

**Tenure.** The total time of holding a post.

**Terminal values.** Refers to those goals that an individual would desire to achieve during his lifetime.

**Terminate at will.** A rule that without a contract the employment relationship can be terminated at will by either the employee or the employer for any reason.

**Termination.** Severing of the employment relationship permanently.

**Termination interview.** An interview in which a worker is informed that he has been dismissed.

**Test.** Any procedure to assess a specific ability.

**Test area.** Geographical area (for example, a city, a district, a town) used for conducting controlled testing. For example, impact of advertising, likeliness of packaging, etc.

**Test group.** A group on which a test is conducted. For example, for knowing the likeliness of a product.

**Test-retest (repetition) method.** A method of determining reliability of a test in which a test is administered twice to the same group of people and correlating the two sets of scores. In other words, a test is given and repeated on same group and the correlation computed between the first and second set of scores. More closer the correlation/reliability coefficient, more reliable the test is considered to be.

**Test validity.** The accuracy with which a test or interview measures what it attempts to measure.

**T-group training.** *See sensitivity training*.

**Thematic appreciation test (TAT).** A projective test in which an individual is asked to describe the situations portrayed in a series of pictures. The themes given by the person indicates his basic personality make up (for example, a city, a district, a town, etc.).

**Theory X**. A negative view of human beings proposed by Douglas Mc Gregor. Under this theory, the assumptions held by managers are that employees inherently dislike work, will avoid responsibilities and seek formal direction, whenever possible, they place security above all other factors and they must be coerced and controlled in order to achieve goals.

**Theory Y.** A positive view of human beings proposed the Douglas Mc Gregor. Under this theory, the assumptions are that employees view work as being as natural as rest or play, they will exercise self-direction and self-control, they seek responsibility and they have ability to make innovative decisions.

**Theory Z.** A theory developed by William Ouchi after making a comparative study of the Japanese and American management practices. According to this theory large complex organisations are human systems and their effectiveness depends on the quality of humanism used. Theory Z represents an integrated model of motivation. Theory Z takes into account the strengths of both Japanese management as well as American management. The letter 'Z' does not stand for anything, it just denotes the state of affairs in an organisation and human behaviour. The main elements are relationship between employees and organisation, employee involvement, integrated organisation, coordination and informal control system.

**Therapy.** A treatment carried out in order to cure a disordered condition.

**Thereblig.** Smallest discreet human motion which can be identified in the performance of a task.

**Third country.** A country other than a parent or a host country.

**Third country nationals (TCNs).** A citizen of one country, working in a second country and employed by the firm headquarted in a third country. For example, an Indian citizen working for a German company in England.

**Three-component model of creativity.** A model which proposes that individual creativity requires expertise, creative-thinking skills and intrinsic task motivation.

**Time and motion study.** A technique for determining the best way of performing a complex task by dividing the task into small steps and then measuring the time taken to perform each small step. In this way, standards of performance are set up and these are used for planning and controlling production work and establishing incentive systems.

**Time card.** A card that records the time spent by a worker at workplace or at a specific job. Also known as **clock card.**

**Time off.** Break from the work given to an employee so that he can attend his private affairs.

**Time rate (time wage) system.** A wage payment system in which wages are paid on the basis of time the employee puts on the work without considering the output of the employee. The wage rates are fixed for an hour, a day, a week, a month, etc. So, the wages are calculated on the basis of attendance. Wages are calculated as: Wages = Number of days/hours worked × Rate per day/hour.

**Time schedule.** Timetable for the total and/or parts of the work.

**Time sheet.** A form which records an employee time or machine time spent on each activity in a specific period.

**Time study.** A method/technique of determining the total time essential to perform a task. This may consists of timing of various elements and then totalling of all the required times and also adding some allowance for things like personal time and fatigue.

**Tip.** A small amount of money given separately and voluntarily to an individual or a group for his or their services.

**Title VII of the civil rights act 1964.** A section of this act which applies to employment decisions makes it unlawful for employers to discriminate against any person with respect to hiring, terms and conditions, compensation, etc. on the basis of religion, sex, race, national origin or colour.

**Token.** A thing which acts as a symbol. For example, as per Factories Act, 1948* the non-adult workers have to carry token while at work, a token gives a reference to their certificate of fitness for such work.

**Token strike (protest strike).** This is a short duration strike with the clear intention of not disrupting the business of the employer but to provide a signal for the danger ahead. This is taken up to communicate the emotions and sentiments of the workers on some matters.

**Top-down programs.** An organisation's efforts to keep all its employees up to date on various matters through intranet postings, e-mail, newsletters, meetings, etc.

**Top management.** A term used to describe those people who are responsible for the overall policy, direction and control of an organisation.

**TOR.** Abbreviation for Technic of Operations Review*.

**Total compensation.** All forms of quantifiable rewards going to employee for his work. It has three main components (i.e., base compensation, pay incentives and indirect compensation/benefits) and the relative proposition of each component in the total compensation varies by the organisation.

**Total disablement.** Means disablement, whether of a temporary or permanent nature, which incapacitates a workman for all work which he was capable of performing at the time of the accident resulting in such disablement.

**Total quality management (TQM).** Means a strategic approach of providing the best to customers through continuous improvements and innovation in all the processes, products and services with the involvement of everybody in the organisation.

**TQM.** Abbreviation for Total Quality Management*.

**Trade association.** A voluntary organisation of members of the same trade or of industry.

**Trade dispute.** *See industrial dispute*.

**Trade publications.** Periodicals (journals, magazines, specific newspapers) dealing with matters of interest to a specific industry or trade.

**Trade union.** An association of employees of a specific trade or industry for the welfare of its members. It will act on its members behalf during collective bargaining. According to Trade Union Act, 1926*, trade union means any combination, whether temporary or permanent, formed (1) primarily for the purpose of regulating the relations

(a) between workmen and employers, or

(b) between workmen and workmen, or

(c) between employers and employers, or

(2) for imposing restrictive conditions on the conduct of any trade or business.

**Training.** A process of teaching new or present employees the basic skills they need to perform their jobs. Helping employees in correcting the deficiencies in their performance.

**Training administration.** Coordination of all the activities before, during and after a training program or session.

**Training design process.** Developing systematically the training programs.

**Training outcomes.** Evaluation of the effectiveness of training program which is based on a skill-based, affective, cognitive and the results outcomes.

**Trait.** Consistent and enduring characteristics of a person. For example, reliability, loyalty, decisiveness, energy, etc.

**Trait appraisal instrument.** An appraisal instrument in which the supervisor/rater makes judgments about workers' traits (like reliability, loyalty, energy, decisiveness). Though a number of firms use trait ratings, however the present opinion is not favourable.

**Trait theories of leadership.** The theories that focus on the personal qualities and characteristics in order to differentiate the leaders from the nonleaders.

**Transaction processing.** Calculations and computations for reviewing and documenting human resource management practices and decisions.

**Transfer of training.** The use of knowledge, skills, abilities (KSAs*) and behaviours learned during training on the job.

**Transfers.** Movement or reassignment of an employee from one job to another with no change in salary, status and responsibilities.

**Transition stay bonus.** The extra payment given to those employees whose jobs are being eliminated. So, in order to motivate them to stay for a period of time in the organisation.

**Transitional matrix.** A matrix that shows number or proportion of employees in the different job categories at different times.

**Transmission machinery.** Means any pulley, system of pulleys, wheel, shaft, drum, clutch, coupling, driving belt or other appliance or device by which the motion of a prime mover is transmitted to or received by a machinery or appliance.

**Transnational corporation.** An organisation having operations in a number of countries. The operations are highly decentralized.

**Transnational process.** Extent to which an organisation's decision-making and planning processes involve the ideas and representatives from different cultures.

**Transnational representation.** The multinational representation or composition of managers in the organisation.

**Transnational scope.** An organisation's capability to make human resource management decisions from an international perspective or view.

**Treasurer.** An individual who is responsible for taking care of money and other assets of a company.

**Trend analysis.** Examining a company's past employment needs over a period of years to estimate the future needs.

**Tribunal.** A court constituted for the settlement of industrial dispute (under adjudication machinery). For example, industrial tribunal, national tribunal.

**Truck.** An earlier method of paying employees in goods rather than cash (cash is presently used method).

**Trust.** A firm belief or confident expectation in the reliability of an individual. In today's organisations, it is an increasingly important leadership issue.

**Trusteeship theory.** *See paternalistic theory.*

**Turnover.** A process of employees leaving the company and they have to be replaced.

**Turnover rate.** The rate of employee separation in a firm.

**Two-factory theory.** *See motivation-hygiene theory.*

**Type A personality.** People with a type A personality aggressively struggle for achieving more and more in a lesser time. They always move, walk and eat rapidly, feel impatient with the rate at which events took place, cannot cope with leisure time, strive to think or do two or more things at one time and obsessed with numbers.

**Type B personality.** A set of personality characteristics just opposite to type A personality. People with a type B personality are causal about their appointment, never feeling rushed, easy-going with a number of interest outside their work, good listeners, slow and deliberate in their manners. Type A and B are extreme instances and generally people lie somewhere between the two.

# U

**Ultimatum.** A warning or statement to a person to threaten him to do or perform something as desired (as per standards) otherwise suitable action will be taken against him.

**Umpire.** A person appointed in an arbitration process when a dispute is referred to an even number of arbitrators. He shall enter upon the reference, in case the arbitrators are equally divided in their opinion and his award shall prevail.

**Unanimous.** When everyone holds the same opinion or everyone votes in the same manner.

**Uncertainty avoidance.** A Geert Hofstede's cultural dimension which describes the extent to which people feel threatened by uncertain situations and they try to avoid them.

**Unclear standards.** Performance appraisal standards which are vague and open that make them difficult to interpret.

**Unconditional.** When no conditions or provisions or terms are attached.

**Unconstitutional strike.** A strike which is called with or without the trade union backing in the area of an agreed procedure.

**Underachiever.** An individual who achieve lesser than he is capable of.

**Underemployment.** A situation in the labour market when people do not have enough work to do. Their skills are not fully utilized in this situation.

**Undermanning.** A situation when lesser number of people are hired than required for the efficient work performance in the organisation.

**Undivided profit.** The profit which has not yet distributed among its shareholders.

**Undue hardship.** A significant difficulty or expense forced upon an employer in making a suitable accommodation for individual with disabilities.

**Unemployment.** A persistent problem in industrial economies in which, even when people actively sought but still they are unable to find work for themselves.

**Unemployment insurance.** A benefit which is given to an individual in case he is unable to find/locate work due to no fault of his own.

**Unfair dismissal.** The dismissal of a worker which an employer cannot prove to be fair.

**Unfair labour practice strike.** A strike through which the illegal conduct of employer is protested.

**Uniform guidelines.** Under U.S. laws, these are the guidelines issued by the federal agencies for ensuring compliance with equal employment federal legislation explaining the recommended employment procedures (regarding matters such as worker selection, pre-employment inquiries, record keeping, etc.) in detail.

**Unilateral.** On one side only.

**Unilateral arbitration.** A situation in which one of the party to industrial dispute decided unilaterally for arbitration as a way for the settlement of industrial dispute.

**Union.** An organisation which represents employees' interests to management on various issues like wages, working conditions, working hours, safety, welfare, etc.

**Union acceptance strategy.** A labour relations strategy in which the management chooses to view union as workers' legimitate representative. It also accepts collective bargaining as mechanism for establishing the workplace rules and regulations.

**Union authorization card.** A card which is signed by a worker in order to designate a union as his collective bargaining agent.

**Union avoidance strategy.** A labour relations strategy in which the management attempts to prevent its workers from joining a union. It is done either by using hardball tactics or by removing the incentive to unionize.

**Union salting.** A trade union organizing tactic in which the full time undercover union organisers are hired by ignorant employers.

**Union security provision.** The contract clauses which aid the union in order to attain and retain the members.

**Union shop.** A form of union security (union arrangement) which requires new employees to join the union in a prescribed period of time (usually 30 to 60 days after their date of hire) and pay dues.

**Union steward.** An employee/advocate who is elected to represent a worker's case to the management in a grievance handling procedure. He serves as the first line representative of the unionized employees.

**Union substitution (Proactive human resource management).** A union avoidance strategy in which the management becomes so responsive to its workers' needs and requirements that it removes/eliminates the incentive for their unionization. Some of the union substitution approaches are like promoting from within, job security, workers participation in management, open door policies and grievance procedure and high involvement practices.

**Union suppression.** A union avoidance strategy in which the management uses hardball tactics (may be legal or illegal) to get rid of a union or to prevent union from organizing its employees at all costs.

**Unit labour cost.** It is calculated by dividing the average cost of employees by their average levels of output.

**Unite.** To join hands or work together for a mission.

**Unity of command.** Means every employee, in an organisation, must receive the orders and be accountable to only one boss. This is essential to avoid the conflicting orders and to ensure stability in the organisation.

**Unity of direction.** Means that there should be one head and one plan for a group of activities having the same objective. It is necessary to ensure the unity and coordination in the organisation.

**Universal concept of management.** A concept of management which holds that all the management practices should be standardised.

**Universe (population).** In statistics, it is the complete set of items which are of interest in any specific situation.

**University of Michigan studies.** The research studies undertaken at the university to locate behavioural characteristics of leaders which appeared to be related to measures of performance effectiveness. The studies identified two dimensions of leadership behaviour i.e., employee-oriented and production-oriented.

**Unmanned manufacturing.** A technology in which the whole manufacturing is done without the help of human operators.

**Unofficial strike.** A strike which takes place without trade union support.

**Unpaid work.** A work carried out/done without any specific pay for this. For example, work of a housewife. This is tough to be assessed in terms of national income.

**Unsafe conditions.** The physical and mechanical conditions in the organisation which can cause accidents.

**Unstructured (non-directive) interview.** An interview in which no set format of questions is followed. The interviewer pursues points of interest as they arise in response to the earlier. The main weakness of this type of interview is that it lacks consistency in assessing candidates.

**Unstructured sequential interview.** An interview in which interviewers may ask the different questions and form an independent opinion.

**Upward communication.** A type of communication which allows the employees at lower levels to communicate their views, feelings and ideas to the higher-level decision-makers.

**Upward feedback.** A performance appraisal process for the managers which includes their subordinates' evaluation.

**Utilitarianism.** A criteria of decision-making in which decisions are made solely on the basis of their consequences or outcomes. This view is consistent with the goals such as maximum profits, productivity and efficiency.

**Utility.** It is the degree to which the information provided by the selection methods enhances the effectiveness of selecting people in the organisations. Generally, the more valid, reliable and generalizable a selection method is, the more utility it will have.

**Utility (cost/benefit) analysis.** An analysis in which statistical or economic models are built in order to identify the costs and benefits associated with specific human resource activities.

**Utilization analysis.** Comparison of the sex, race and ethnic composition of an organisation's workforce with that of the available labour supply in the market. For example, in case the percentage of the organisation's workforce (like female) is much less than the percentage of the comparison group, then minority group is considered as underutilized.

**Utilization review.** A review and audit of the costs and services billed by the health care providers for second opinion. It is done to ensure that no service is provided unnecessary or deliberately overcharged or incorrectly billed.

# V

**Vacancy.** A job in the organisation which is required to be filled.

**Vacation.** A period (or holiday) when persons are not working in organisation.

**Valid.** Sound or true or which have legal force.

**Validity.** The extent to which a measurement technique measures what it is designed to measure (i.e. behaviour, phenomenon or activity). In case of selection, it is the extent to which scores on a test or interview correlate with actual performance on job.

**Value chain analysis.** An analysis which involves identification of the key or primary activities which create value for the customers and the related supporting activities.

**Value survey.** A tool which is used to help a person in identifying and clarifying the priorities of his value system.

**Value system.** A hierarchy formed by the ranking of a person's values in terms of their intensity. Ranking of an individual's values in terms of their intensity. It is identified by the relative importance a person assign to values like self-respect, honesty, equality, pleasure, faithfulness and freedom.

**Values.** Represent basic convictions that a specific mode of conduct is personally and socially preferable than the opposite ones. Refer to an individual's ideas about what is good, desirable or right.

**Variable.** A product's (or service's) characteristic which can be measured on a continuous variable scale like time, length, etc.

**Variable factor programming.** A concept which is based on the principle that it is a management function to determine what constitutes a fair day's work, assign work and control its flow.

**Variable-interval reinforcement schedule.** A reinforcement schedule which distributes rewards in time in such a manner that reinforcements become unpredictable.

**Variable-pay program.** A pay program in which a portion of employee's pay/ salary is based on some individual and/or organisational measure of performance. For example, profit sharing, gain sharing, bonuses, piece-rate plans and wage incentives.

**Verbal.** The use of spoken words only (no written communication).

**Verbal comprehension.** An individual's capacity to understand and use the spoken and written language.

**Vertical communication.** An upward or downward communication in an organisation.

**Vestibule training (Vestibule school).** A type of training which is preliminary to actual shop experience, the shop conditions are duplicated but instruction is the major objective not the output. The advantage of this type of in-service training is specialization.

**Vesting.** A provision/guarantee in which the money placed in a pension fund will be given to the plan participants on retirement or when they leave the employer and cannot be forfeited for any reason.

**Veteran.** An employee who has been on the same post or position for so many years (a well-experienced person).

**Vicarious liability.** Liability of an employer for employees actions when they are working under given instructions.

**Victimization.** Unfair treatment of an employee either by his employer or by peers.

**Videoconferencing.** A system which enables people at different locations to see and speak to each other. It makes possible to hold conferences, meetings, etc. without travelling at far locations.

**Vietnam era veteran's readjustment assistance act of 1974.** A U.S. act which requires the employers with government contracts take affirmative action to employ disabled veterans and qualified veterans of the Vietnam era.

**Vigilance.** An individual's capability to perform a task with a constant level of efficiency and effectiveness over a period of time.

**Vigilance decrement.** Refer to a decline in an individual's capability to perform a given task with a constant level of efficiency and effectiveness over a period of time. This may due to the fact that individual becomes tired or not able to respond because of the psychological factors.

**Violate.** To break an agreement or a rule.

**Virtual reality (VR).** Use of number of computer-base technologies to create a replica of an entire real-life working environment rather than just several aspects of it like in simulation*.

**Virtual team.** A team that uses computer technology (like wide-area network, e-mail, videoconferencing*) to tie together its physically dispersed members to attain a common objective and goal.

**Vocational guidance.** A branch of the field of occupational psychology that helps/guides the people in selecting/choosing a career or an occupation. This sort of guidance benefits the people along with their prospective employers. This involves the use of various psychological tests like aptitude tests, interest tests, etc. and an interview.

**Vocational rehabilitation act, 1973.** A U.S. act which requires certain federal contractors to take affirmative action in employing handicapped person.

**Vocational training.** A training for a specific trade, profession or business.

**Voice mail.** A type of electronic communication which allows the sender to leave a detailed voice message for the receiver.

**Voicing.** A formal way of complaining about one's work situation.

**Voluntary bargaining items.** Those items in collective bargaining which are neither mandatory nor illegal. These items become a part of negotiations by joint agreement of both labour and management. Neither party can compel the other party to negotiate against its wishes on those items.

**Voluntary reduction in pay plan.** An alternative approach to layoffs in which all the workers agree for the reductions in their salary in order to keep everyone working in the organisation.

**Voluntary separation.** A separation which occurs when a worker decides to end the relationship with the employer for some personal or professional reasons.

**Voluntary time off.** An alternative approach to layoffs in which some of the workers agree to take sometime off in order to reduce the management's payroll and avoid the need for a layoff.

**Voluntary turnover.** Employee turnover* initiated by the workers in an organisation.

**Voluntary welfare.** All those welfare activities which are undertaken by the employers at their own. For example, provisions of medical, educational, transport, housing facilities.

**Volunteer.** A person who willingly offers to do something.

**Vote.** To give or show your opinions/ views/preferences by raising your hand or put a mark on a paper. During elections, to inform who want to be elected.

**VR.** Abbreviation for Virtual Reality*.

# W

**Wage and salary survey.** A survey of what other organisations are paying for the various jobs in the industry and/or area.

**Wage curve.** A curve which shows the relationship between the value of the job and the average wage paid to this job.

**Wage differentials.** The differences in the salaries between employees with different skills in the same industry or between employees with almost similar skills in different industries. The common types of wage differentials are occupational or skill differentials, geographic wage differentials and differentials on the basis of age or sex.

**Wage freeze.** A government's effort to counter (control) inflation by fixing the wages at their existing level for a specific period.

**Wage restraint.** A measure to control prices in which trade union agreement is obtained regarding making only the necessary claims for wage rises. It is less rigid in application as compared to wage freeze*.

**Wages.** These are the payments which are directly calculated on the amount of time worked on the job. Regular payments to an employee for the work done.

**Wages council.** A body established in order to determine the level of wages within a particular industry.

**Wagner act (National Labor Relations Act, 1935).** A U.S. act which is designed to protect the employees' rights to form and join trade unions and to engage in activities like collective bargaining, picketing and strikes.

**Waiting time.** A time period during which the machine operators (or machinery itself) lying idle. They are waiting for the material or work itself.

**Walsh-Healey public contract act, 1936.** A U.S. act which requires minimum wage and working conditions for those workers who are working on any government contract amounting to be more than $ 10,000.

**Wards Cove v. Atonio.** A decision of U.S. Supreme Court involving an Alaska fishery which makes it difficult to prove a case of unlawful discrimination against an employer.

**WARN.** Abbreviation for Worker Adjustment and Retraining Notification Act, 1988*.

**Warning.** Verbal or written message to a worker informing some punishment or dismissal in case, in future, the performance or behaviour is not up to the desired standards.

**Wastage.** In context of human resources, it refers to losing employees when they retire or resign and not when are dismissed.

**Watchdog body.** A body (usually a government office, judiciary) which keep an eye so that all rules and regulations are followed.

**Weed out.** To remove the undesirable and unsuitable applicants.

**Week.** Means a period of 7 days beginning at midnight on Saturday night or such other night as may be approved in writing for a specific area by the chief inspector of factories.

**Welfare.** In context with labour it means anything done for the physical, moral, economic and intellectual betterment of employees, whether by their organisations, or government or any other agency.

**Welfare officer.** A person appointed to protect the workers from the malpractices of the industry and improve labour administration in the factories. As per Factories Act, 1948*, in every factory*, wherein 500 or more workers are employed, the employer shall employ such number of welfare officers as may be prescribed.

**Well paid.** An individual who is paid good or high salary.

**Well pay.** This is the extra pay for not taking the sick leave.

**Well qualified.** An individual who possess good qualifications for a job.

**Wellness program.** An organisation sponsored program which focuses on preventing the employees health problems. It guides employers about the benefits of exercise and good nutrition. It helps them in the identification of potential health risks through testing.

**Whistle-blower.** A person who reveal (or report) the unethical or illegal practices of his employer to the outsiders (for example, media, government agencies).

**Whistle blowing.** It is an employee's disclosure about his employer's illegitimate, illegal or immoral practices to the media, government, organisations or persons who may be able to take the appropriate and corrective action.

**White collar crime.** The crime committed by office people like fund embezzlement.

**White collar union.** A trade union of white collar employees (officers).

**White collar worker.** A worker working in an office and not in a factory (i.e., manual job).

**Whole life policy.** A type of endowment policy in which the proceeds of the policy are given after the death of the assured person, whenever that happens.

**Wholly owned subsidiary.** In international business, it is a foreign branch of a company which is fully owned by the home country's office.

**Wildcat strike.** An unauthorized and spontaneous strike which is suddenly announced. In this, workers go on a strike without any notice or at very short notice. Usually, this type of strike take place due to some provocation and the real cause may be some other fundamental issue between employees and employer.

**Withdraw.** To take back the offer given earlier.

**Witness.** Observer of an actual event and who can provide evidence that it has actually takes place.

**Word association test.** A projective test in which the candidate is required to state some words, feeling and objects associated with the given word.

**World-wide web (www).** An internet service which provides browser software allowing users to explore the various items on the web.

**Work.** The effort (physical and mental) put in order to achieve the results.

**Work day.** A day when the work is performed (opposite to a holiday).

**Work design.** A sub-part of the total job design process which is concerned with the actual working operations (in opposition to the human resource management aspects).

**Work experience.** Total time period spent doing work in a company.

**Work flow.** The way in which the work is organised in order to meet the company's production or service goals.

**Work flow analysis.** Study of how the work creates or adds value to the outgoing processes in a company's business. Examining the way the work (i.e., the inputs, activities, outputs) moves through the firm.

**Work group.** A group which interacts primarily, to share information and to make decisions to help each member of the group perform within his area of responsibility. A work group have no opportunity to engage in a collective work which require joint effort i.e., no positive synergy.

**Workload.** The total amount of work which an individual has to do in the organisation.

**Workman.** A person who performs/ work with his hands.

**Work measurement.** A technique of establishing the time required for a worker to finish a specific task at a desired level of performance.

**Workplace.** The place where the employees work.

**Work practices.** Set ways of performing the work. These may develop from traditional way of doing work and this limits the job design. Sometimes, these practices become a part of trade union-management relationship.

**Work rules.** The terms and conditions of employment including salary, work assignments, grievance handling procedures, vacations and rest breaks.

**Work samples.** The real or actual work/job tasks used in testing the candidates' performance.

**Work sampling technique/tests.** A testing method which is based on the concept of measuring performance on the actual basic job tasks.

**Work sharing.** An alternative approach to layoffs in which a group of employees agrees for a temporary reduction in work hours during the economic downturns.

**Work simplification.** An approach to job design in which the work is broken down into simple and repetitive tasks that maximize efficiency. It utilizes worker effectively in order to produce a larger amount of standardized product. However, this approach often results in boredom, low satisfaction and turnover.

**Work station.** The physical environment where the job is performed.

**Work study technique.** A demand forecasting technique in which volume of workload for the forthcoming years are analysed and on this basis, analysis of personnel requirement is done. Allowances are also made for absenteeism, labour turnover, idle time, etc. Also known as **workload analysis.**

**Work team.** A group that generates positive synergy through the coordinated effort i.e., individual efforts result in a performance which is greater than the sum of individual inputs.

**Work-to-rule.** A type of strike in which the workers perform the work literally in accordance with the rules or procedures laid down for the purpose. The employees follow the rules of work in such a manner that they result in dislocation of work.

**Worker.** Means a person employed, directly or by or through any agency (including a contractor) with or without the knowledge of the principal employer. The person may be employed for or without remuneration.

**Worker adjustment and retraining notification act (WARN), 1988.** A U.S. act which requires U.S. employers having 100 or more employees to give 60 days' advance notice to employee who will be laid off as a result of a plant closing or a mass separation of 50 or more employees.

**Workers' compensation.** A legal provision of medical care and benefits and income to the job-related accident victims or their dependents regardless of their fault.

**Workers participation in management (WPM).** A concept of industrial democracy that indicates an effort on the part of an employer to create a system of communication for informing employee, either formally or informally about the organisation's affairs and through this system, the employees also express their opinions and suggestions.

**Workforce diversity.** Refers to organisations becoming more heterogeneous in terms of race, gender, ethnicity and nationality.

**Workforce utilization review.** A comparison of the percentage or proportion of employees in the protected sub-groups with the percentage or proportion which each sub-group represents in the labour market.

**Work-in-strike.** A type of strike in which the employees refuse to leave the workplace and keep on performing their work, although usually the management instruct them not to perform.

**Workmen's compensation act, 1923.** An act that provides for the payment of compensation by employers to their workmen in case of an accident as a measure of relief and social security. The theory of workmen's compensation states that "the cost of product should bear the blood of the workmen". Passing of this act was the first step towards social security of workmen in India. The act enables a workman to get compensation irrespective of his negligence.

**Works Committee.** A committee constituted under Industrial Disputes Act, 1947*, to encourage voluntary settlement of disputes, to remove causes of friction between the employers and workmen in the day-to-day working and to promote measures for securing amity and good relations between them. Any industrial establishment where 100 or more workmen are employed then the employer is required to constitute a works committee consisting of equal representatives of employers and workmen.

**Works council.** A committee or a group of nominated or elected workers who must be consulted, whenever management makes decisions involving personnel. For example, in a case of merger, the management must inform the works council at an early stage.

**WPM.** Abbreviation for Workers Participation in Management*.

**Write in.** A written enquiry from the outside of the company about whether any jobs are available or not.

**Wrongful discharge.** A worker's dismissal which does not comply with the contractual arrangement stated or implied by the company in its employment application forms or which does not comply with the law. Termination of a worker for illegal or inappropriate reasons.

**WWW.** Abbreviation for World Wide Web*.

# Y

**Yield ratio.** A comparison of the number of candidates at the one stage of the recruitment process to the number of candidates at the next stage.

**Young person.** Means a person who is either a child or an adolescent.

# Z

**Zero defect.** An employee motivational technique which is designed to improve quality. It encourages error-free (i.e., zero defect) performance in organisation.

**Zero sum game.** In game theory, it is a game in which one party/player's gains are exactly equals the other's losses. One party's gain at the expense of other's.